THEME and VARIATIONS

THEME and VARIATIONS
Cautionary Tales of a 2nd Violin

PETER MARKHAM

THIRSTY BOOKS
EDINBURGH
& PITTENWEEM

© Peter Markham 2024

Published by Thirsty Books 2024

www.thirstybooks.com

The author has asserted his moral rights.

British Library Cataloguing-in-Publication Data.
A catalogue record for this book is available from the British Library.

ISBN 978 1 7393181 2 3 hardback

Design and typeset by
derek.rodger21@outlook.com

Cover
Tangletree Designs

Printed by
Bell & Bain Ltd, Glasgow

For all those who have contributed to making my life
in the music profession rich in unforgettable entertainment,
both given and received – and as a warning for my four
granddaughters that things don't always turn out as one expects.

But when some pipsqueak takes up his pen as the evening lengthens – well full marks for gall! And the remainder shops do deserve our full support.

– Martin Amis, *London Fields*

FOREWORD

JAMES NAUGHTIE

Music is a human business. For each moment of the sublime, there are hours of workaday labour and, frequently, emotional chaos. The joy of Peter Markham's memoir is his candid picture of life off-stage, rendered with the ease of a natural storyteller, which meanders through bars, late-night parties and schoolboyish escapades on nearly every continent, as well as into serious hours in dry rehearsal rooms or alone with a solitary violin at home.

His travels with that fiddle will ring true to amateur and professional musicians alike, because he makes the point tellingly that experiences can be uncommonly similar in a village hall in Orkney or a vast opera house in some distant capital. He won't forget the one in Madrid where he took his place as a member of the Edinburgh Quartet on an otherwise empty stage and discovered that, having left his score in the wings, he had to navigate a narrow door in the towering backdrop and retrieve it, before making the long, lonely walk back to his music stand in order to begin to play.

Throughout his often hilarious account of life in the Ulster Orchestra, the Northern Sinfonia, and the Edinburgh Quartet itself (for more than two decades as second violin) there's the sound of that poignant note. His own incurable stage fright (the kind of revelation that would stun an audience gripped by a performance), and the inevitable tempests that spring up when the talents of creative folk are let loose on each other backstage. How could it be otherwise? They want to play together, but they also want to be themselves. The intimacy of music-making sometimes comes at a price.

Of course, it's full of fun. The strains of a performance, whether it goes well or ill, are so often relieved by the sheer verve of life on the road, violin-case in hand. Anyone picking up this book will, I'm sure, find reassurance in the knowledge that the urge to play, to listen, and to perform is embedded in so many people that it simply cannot be suppressed, however intimidating and corrosive the efforts of some arts administrators and accountants may be. This is a story of survival: how the music, and the players, can see it through. And usually, with gusto – even after one of the long bacchanalian nights that, in Peter's experience, punctuate the working days of any orchestra, or even quartet, when it departs from home base.

A joyous romp, mostly. But underneath, of course, is the story of a commitment to music that's unshakeable. A young man, of resolute beliefs and political views, discovers the violin and prospers, because he loves it. He studies and trains with passion, and sets off on the sometimes perilous path to a professional career. In the years that follow we learn a great deal about the character behind the music stand – his loves and jealousies, and his natural bond with the infinite arrangements of notes that first captivated him as a youngster. In this story, he hardly needs to describe the effect of music on his emotions and his mind: it is obvious on every page.

That is how it should be. Not music as an objective influence, somewhere out there, but music running into every corner of a life. Always there, always working some kind of magic. His is a story to treasure.

Theme and Variations

PROLOGUE

On rainy weekends as a child, library books read and daytime television and the internet yet to rear their intrusive heads, I was frequently drawn to an encyclopaedia of photographs caged in the glass-fronted bookcase in our mostly unused front room. Two photos from those days are still firmly etched in my memory, one of the Forth Railway Bridge, and the other of Hungarians playing chess whilst immersed up to their waists in a thermal spa pool in Budapest. From that point all things Hungarian randomly impinged upon my life: a couple of pages of highly coloured and unusually shaped stamps in my stamp album; news of the 1956 revolution; universal adulation of Messi-like Puskas; and an inspirational violin teacher called Vilmos Schummy. Now in my late seventies, impingement has become saturation. I live there.

Between bidding and playing *ketto treff* or *harom szan*, or any other contract, the four of us pepper our weekly bridge evening with chat and gentle banter. Boglárka has been known to ask more than once, 'Peter, would you ever have imagined that you would end up living in Szeged?'

Thirty plus years ago, Bogi – this diminutive form has no vulgar connotations in Hungary; quite the opposite, Boglárka is the Hungarian for buttercup – had been an *au pair* for my children in Edinburgh but now, with her husband János, and my wife Sára, we make up the bridge four.

Since 1989 Bogi and I had always kept in touch through an exchange of Christmas cards, then in 2007 she wrote saying her father had just died, and that it would be nice to see me if I could find time to visit her in Hungary. I duly booked a flight to Hungary for the July and informed Bogi of this by email finishing with the casual remark, 'So that gives you three months to find me a Hungarian wife.'

For the four days of my subsequent visit Bogi had organised a comprehensive itinerary beginning with a barbeque in her garden on the first evening. Present would be Bogi's family, her mother, brother and family, and a close friend called Sára – I had now met my bridge partner and future wife!

Szeged is a delightfully sedate and compact city in the south of Hungary close to borders with both Romania and Serbia, a city boasting a multitude of Art Nouveau and Art Deco architecture, and a profusion of pavement cafes. Almost immediately on arriving there for that holiday in 2007 my eyes lit upon a poster advertising a concert by the local orchestra, the Szeged Symphony Orchestra. The conductor's name, written in bold letters was none other than János Furst, ex-Leader of the Ulster Orchestra, the orchestra in which my professional career had begun in 1966 as Sub-Leader. János had given up playing in 1969, preferring a more brightly lit life than that of a common orchestral player.

The poster was well out of date and as I was soon to discover, János had died a month or so before I arrived, ending his days as principal conductor of the Szeged Symphony Orchestra.

So, this is as good a time as any to chart the intervening years between Northern Ireland and my present domicile in Hungary, and impart a few random truths about a life in classical music.

Theme and Variations

ONE

At the outset, any serious musician will ensure they have the appropriate parentage in place to kick-start and maintain their art and career. That was my first mistake...

As a violinist of no particular eminence or distinction, it is obvious and inescapable that responsibility for this lack of world-shattering celebrity and everything else that unfolds in the coming pages lies entirely in the hands of my parents. I refuse to let them off the hook and therefore to better understand why I have turned out as I have, I am compelled to begin by detailing my family background at some length.

It was quite clear to see how my mother's placid role as a 24-hour mum played a major part in giving me and my siblings a warm, loving and safe home while my humourless and emotionally inhibited father contented himself in hunting and gathering to enable mum's success. The household revolved around my mother because dad worked *nights* as he put it, meaning we only met in passing; my arrival home from school followed his departure one hour later. This limited contact did not however stop him from being the greater presence.

Born in 1910, Alfred Jesse was a bundle of contradictions. He was also my father, father foremost, dad partially. He died when I was forty-three and he seventy-eight. Throughout his life he had often quoted 'Man hath but three score years and ten' and, on passing the age of seventy, he viewed any extension as an unwanted bonus. He then spent those final eight years just hanging about miserably, waiting for the inevitable to happen, determined that the prediction of Psalms 90 should hold true. My father either chose to ignore, or it failed to register that the biblical quotation goes on to suggest that although living to seventy is all we should expect, making it to eighty is a realistic possibility. He also ignored the fact that longevity has increased dramatically in the last two thousand years.

Paradoxically, when the time came for him to depart this world, he stubbornly fought to stay alive. Hospitalised in the final weeks of his life, his herculean efforts to leave the bed in his then feeble condition were so physical, he was moved to a room by himself with his mattress laid directly on the floor, as launching himself out of bed and crashing dangerously to the tiles below was something he was becoming quite accomplished at. This manifestation of his mental anguish was an unexpected coda at the end of his life, coming as a complete contradiction to his asserted belief in his preordained demise.

He was a miserable 'old git' to use his own words, a reference he reserved for other people. His general demeanour was quiet and serious, rarely showing joy about anything. His most obvious display of contentment was when curled up on the front room sofa each afternoon with Turpin, the small family dog, listening to classical music from his vast collection of LPs on his cherished radiogram. (Turpin was named after Randolph Turpin the middleweight boxer, because it was thought that this mongrel pup would grow to be boxer-like in appearance as he had been fathered by a thoroughbred: he failed dismally but was loved by all.)

The radiogram was my father's pride and joy and after the upright piano, the dominant piece of furniture in our front room. Replacement of the simple gramophone by this monstrous piece of equipment was extremely popular in the 1950s and 60s and I suspect owned as much for its reassuring presence in bestowing a sense of comfort and achievement as for its primary function.

As was common at the time, my father left school in 1924 at the age of fourteen and soon after began a seven-year apprenticeship as a stereo typist in the newspaper industry. Proudly embarking on his apprenticeship seemed to sow the seeds for this fourteen-year-old brother of six older sisters to better himself in all sorts of ways – although I believe he was always frustrated that he never fulfilled his real potential.

He enrolled in a gymnasium specialising in *Physical Culture*. One of the techniques he mastered was the ability to roll his abdominal muscles up and down his abdomen like the ripples on the beach of a gently receding tide and would proudly finish every demonstration by aligning his abdominals in a rigid, perpendicular formation. He was still able to perform this feat with immense pride well into his sixties. He also signed up to an evening class to learn German, becoming competent enough to hold a conversation in the language. Once, during World War Two, the bus on which he was travelling came to an abrupt halt, two policemen boarded, removed my father and marched him off to a police station. The action had been prompted by an overzealous passenger on the same bus reporting that a possible German spy was on board having earlier observed my father reading a German language textbook.

I think these efforts, both physical and intellectual were motivated by a desire to move from a background of trade to that of the intelligentsia and so he decided to embark on a comprehensive form of home-schooling. Alongside learning German, he read voraciously. Newspapers in the form of the *Daily Herald*, *Reynold's News* and of course *Peace News*. I couldn't be sure he ever read every volume of Dickens resting in the front room bookcase, but as he was wont to quote from various volumes, he must have given it a good go. The shelves supported an eclectic mix of subjects besides novels, books on painters, architecture, history, biography including *A Pattern of Islands, The Kon-Tiki Expedition, The Riddle of The Sands*. Poetry was also well represented. Throughout dad's entire life, he carried an edition of the *Rubaiyat of Omar Khayyam* in his jacket pocket. I still have that battered copy.

My father was a practising Quaker and member of the Peace Pledge Union and a staunch pacifist, so when the war erupted, taking up arms was not an option. Instead, after appearing before a tribunal to prove he was a genuine conscientious objector, he was legally required to undertake necessary community work for the duration of the war and this he did by working as a surveyor for the War Agricultural Department in Norfolk. Although this was local work, enabling him to live at home in Norwich, it was far from being the ideal state of affairs one might imagine. The risk of losing his life was all but removed in comparison to those in the armed forces but being at home each night with his wife and daughter, when most of the men who lived in the street were risking their lives hundreds of miles away, came with a separate set of issues.

Hughenden Road in Norwich was built around 1900, a tightly packed, one-hundred-and-fifty-metre-long cul-de-sac of terraced housing ending at a railway cutting. My mother's parents also lived on the street as did one of her cousins and his family and another Quaker family, who were my parents' closest friends, Jack and Merle Boddy. (Jack later became General Secretary of the now defunct National Union of Agricultural and Allied Workers.) Pacifism garners little sympathy at the best of times so it's easy to imagine the attention, interest and animosity that surrounded the two Quaker families and their relatives living in this close-knit community in the midst of the mighty conflict and genocide that was World War Two.

My father made little or no mention of this discomfort in the years after the war, but my mother when asked about the six long war years, would recount with great unhappiness the trials and tribulations of bringing up my sister Elizabeth, born in 1937. My mother was ostracized and socially isolated by neighbours who wouldn't allow their children to mix with my sister, so apart from family and Quaker friends, it must have seemed like a form of solitary confinement.

A number of years later, against all the odds, I acquired a toy gun. Even my father's pacifism wasn't powerful enough to deny me this model firearm, which must have been a concession to a small child's need for acceptance among his peers. The compromise wasn't entirely devoid of influence as he did insist that my toy gun should look as little like a modern weapon as possible, so I became the proud owner of a pirate's flintlock. Alongside this flintlock, a few Dinky toy vehicles of a military theme were allowed, but an even more glaring contradiction was yet to come.

My mother was an only child and pampered rotten by her parents. Most Sundays, the three would dress in their finest clothes and take a ride in a landau, simply as a treat. Throughout her life she reminded us children of how much she was attached to her father and how much she missed him when he was at the front in the Great War. She frequently mentioned gifts he had brought back for her whilst serving in Africa in various campaigns, an ostrich feather being one of her most precious keepsakes. This was carefully wrapped in tissue paper and safely stashed away in a drawer until the day she died. She always remembered in which drawer to find it and would relish the chance to show it to anyone she thought might be interested when the appropriate moment arose. Reminiscing about her father was always imbued with a great deal of affection and a keen sense of pride.

I have a photo from my primary school days, taken at a

Fancy dress party at primary school, 1954

fancy-dress party one Christmas and prominently positioned front and centre is a little boy in military dress uniform. The child dutifully saluting is me! The bright red and black tunic with broad white belt and black Glengarry style cap had been lovingly made by my mother in unconscious (or perhaps not) homage to her adored father and I had the honour of wearing it as her adored elder son. I never learned my mother's true feelings on pacifism, or her political sympathies, but my wearing of this uniform seemed the closest she ever overtly came to proclaiming her own allegiances in contradiction to my father. It was not the only outing the uniform got either; I remember wearing it on at least two other occasions around this time and have no memory of my father raising any objection.

By the time I arrived, two months after the cessation of hostilities in 1945, remarkably, the street had returned to something close to normality. Our family and friends felt no great urgency to move from the area and any enmity of the previous six years subsided as the community came together again in its efforts to rebuild a society no longer at war.

It wasn't only within the local community that efforts were made to put the world back together on a more caring basis. By the end of 1946, there were still 400,000 prisoners of war, (POWs) in Britain and non-fraternisation rules meant that they had been confined to prison for a year and a half since the end of the war, only being allowed outside the prison walls when they were engaged in menial work for the government. But Christmas of 1946 saw a relaxation of this rule and British families were able to invite up to three POWs to their homes for Christmas lunch. This was an attempt to build bridges and help normalise life for both parties. My parents eagerly offered lunch to two POWs, Heinrich and Hans and from that Christmas lunch, as the easing of the non-fraternisation restrictions became ever looser, a friendship developed with both men and eventually their families. One of the men, Heinrich, became a close friend and from the time of his repatriation in 1947 and for the following twenty years, every Christmas a large parcel from Germany would arrive, containing traditional fare: tins of homemade *schweinekopfsulze* (pork head cheese), gingerbread, chocolate and a sparkly nativity card which shed most of its glitter in the post. The friendship continued well after my father's death, ending sixty-eight-years later in 2014 on the death of my mother at one hundred-and-three.

Over the years, my parents and Heinrich and his wife made several visits to each other's homes, with the last occurring

Heinrich (r) arriving in Norfolk, with the author and his father, 1987

when Heinrich and one of his granddaughters, visited my mother shortly before her one hundredth birthday in Swaffham.

In 1948 we left Norwich and moved to the suburbs of London. We were by then a family of five as I had acquired a brother Tony, born in 1948. The move was precipitated by my father's search for work in his trade as a stereo typist. I think it had dawned on him by then that he was unlikely to ever fulfil his ambition of pursuing a more intellectual career (ideally, something rooted in politics) and so, frustratingly, settled for a lifetime in the newspaper industry. His dream of an alternative existence as a politician mostly remained alive in front of the television in the living-room, as an armchair socialist, though angry unbridled expression of his left-wing views could make unexpected appearances.

Many years later, my mother used to tell a story about a five-hour long train journey she and my father made, to visit me in Edinburgh where I was living at the time. They board the train at Peterborough and find themselves seated in one of those configurations where couples sit opposite each other separated by a shared table. As the train departs Peterborough, with my parents settling comfortably in place and preparing to get stuck into their various reading matter, my mother mutters to my father that she has forgotten her book and has nothing to read. This information is picked up by the elderly couple opposite and the man instantly slides his newspaper across the table saying, 'Please, have my paper, I've finished reading it.'

Unfortunately, this publication falls into the category of

Tory propaganda as far as my father is concerned and before my mother has time to react, my father propels the *Daily Telegraph* back in the direction from whence it came, accompanied by, 'She doesn't want to read that Tory rubbish!'

My mother is mortified. Mortified for five hours.

Instigating this type of situation came without a flicker of remorse to follow. Once his intolerance had been unleashed and his moral indignity satisfied, his behaviour would return to normal and he would appear to be oblivious to the discomfort and offence he had just caused to all those within earshot. Naturally enough, my long-suffering mother was affected most of all and we children, at an early age, soon learnt the meaning of the word 'embarrassment'.

My mother was less affected by the social repercussions of my father's pacifism than by his intolerance and insistence at any given moment, of demonstrating his political views. Within the home it could be an outburst at the television, prompted by news items or adverts promulgating consumerism, or attacking a complete stranger over a barking dog. I can never remember mum expressing political views of her own, perhaps she was too preoccupied shoring up the damage incurred by dad's insensitive declarations of principle: putting things right with offended neighbours, apologising to her circle of social acquaintances and generally defusing awkward moments. This was more than enough motivation to keep her views to herself. I'm certain she would have invited a lot more people to the house had the dread of an Alf eruption not been ever present.

As dad worked nights, her role as a stay-at-home mum

entailed administering to the family needs twenty-four-hours-a-day, five-days-a-week and as an extra concern, she had to keep a careful eye on dad's management of his Type 1 diabetes. It was common practice for her to force-feed him with glucose to stop him slipping into a coma, or to have to ring for an ambulance because he was already comatose. She found this a constant worry. Amazingly, she did have a life outside the family, attending classes in handicrafts and producing work she would proudly display on completion. She was also a volunteer helper for the Mind organization. Why she chose this particular charity was unclear, although Hilda, one of dad's sisters had undergone electroconvulsive therapy in her later years.

Our annual seaside summer holiday and the advent of the transistor radio in the Fifties was not a happy combination. We always knew what was in store, as dad could terrorise a beach in much the same way as a rabid drill sergeant might torment his raw recruits. Once at the beach and after trudging what would seem like an eternity, a suitable spot as far away from humanity would be claimed. He would then seek out any radios within audible range and order they be silenced. This was not always successful, to tell the truth it was hardly ever successful, often resulting in an aggressive exchange of expletives and the Markham family upping sticks and moving even further along the beach, until a final resting place could be achieved, accompanied only by the less intrusive screeching of seagulls and the calming effect of a gently lapping sea. I reckon we walked most of the British coastline in our attempts to avoid the dreaded transistor radio.

Maybe these confrontational and uncompromising episodes were a clear sign that his nascent ambition to enter the world of politics could only have ended in disaster. His prejudices were many and eclectic: Royalty – parasites; Religion – full of hypocrisy (Quakerism had been left far behind by this point); Capitalism – the worship of money; Money – the root of all evil (another biblical misquotation). But his most loathsome bigotry was reserved for the Tories and the Jewish race. At some point in his life, he seems to have been drawn into believing international conspiracy theories that attribute the cause of most of the ills of the world at the door of the Jews, in particular the plight of the poor and working class. It was irrational, unreasonable, blinkered and completely out of kilter with his professed belief in the brotherhood of *all* mankind.

Could the misery he suffered throughout his life have been self-inflicted because he held such extreme views?

In 1967, during my first year as a professional violinist, I explored the possibility of taking up a position in three orchestras, one of which was the Haifa Symphony Orchestra. On informing my father of my thoughts by letter, his reply was speedy and truly remarkable.

> 'About your going to Haifa – I would neither attempt
> to persuade or dissuade you; it's one of those
> increasing number of decisions you'll have to think
> over, sleep on, ponder again and decide for yourself.
> Any thoughts I have on it crystallize round the fact of
> the simply enormous talent, particularly musical talent

that resides in the Jewish race. Think of the composers and performers – it's a lengthy and formidable list. In other aspects of your life to live and work in the atmosphere of the new state of Israel could, in my belief, be a tremendous experience and inspiration. There is one thing to remember – it is very hot out there and the heat doesn't suit you. Forgive me for reminding you.'

He had been a member of Norwich Cathedral Choir as a young man and had no time for any musical genre other than 'Classical Music'. The one exception was anything sung by Paul Robeson, spirituals or excerpts from *Porgy and Bess*. This I'm sure, was due as much to political empathy as musical admiration, as Robeson was one of very few black singers at the time, to have been accepted in the 'serious' music world, or indeed, any other world. My father was very outspoken on racial inequality, especially that of the black man and the apartheid regime of South Africa. The contradictions mount up.

Beethoven was my father's favourite composer and Beethoven's third symphony, the great 'Eroica', my father's favourite piece.

A phone call at 4 a.m. is never going to be good news as is the case on this morning in 1988. Although it is anticipated and comes as no surprise, the death of my father in Kings Lynn is sad news. As I'm living three-hundred miles away in Edinburgh, there is nothing to be done at this early hour and I return to bed to try and sleep out what remains of the night.

In the morning, my partner Niamh (also a violinist) and I, keep the news from our two children and put the family routine into action: children readied and delivered to school, Niamh, to a day of rehearsing with the Scottish Chamber Orchestra and me, to a morning-only rehearsal with the Edinburgh Quartet, of which I was a member. This means that my rehearsal allows me to be back home to an empty house by lunchtime, giving me time and circumstance to reflect and absorb the news of my father's death.

Since the age of twenty-two I have lived with back problems and relish any opportunity to lie flat on my back rather than sit. I now do this on the living-room floor in front of a large wooden trunk on which the radio sits. My intention is to accompany my reflections with whatever music emerges from Radio 3, a deliberate attempt not to influence my emotions by resorting to personal choice. I sit up briefly, depress the on button and lie back down. Nothing happens, not a sound.

I wait a few seconds and decide to try again. Sitting up, I lean forward but just before my finger reaches the radio, it comes to life. I *had* depressed the button fully and the silence had been the result of an inordinately long gap between movements of a symphony. As I resume my prone position, I am overtaken by a sense of confusion and overwhelming grief at what I hear. It's a slow movement, but not any old slow movement. It's *Marcia Funebre* from Beethoven's *Eroica*, his third symphony!

This must be one of the most cathartic moments in my life as the tears flow freely in waves of sorrow and incomprehension. What a way for my dad to say goodbye. Since that day I have been more open to the inexplicable surrounding us all.

TWO

When presented with a choice of instruments to learn, the aspiring professional musician will choose the silliest one available. I got this bit right.

My mother was an only child, but together with my father and his six sisters (there were two brothers, one died at birth and the other from diphtheria aged seventeen), the larger family added up to a sizeable clan. However, my father's membership of Norwich Cathedral Choir was the family's only expression of a more than usual interest in music; that is until my brother and I came along.

Both my younger brother and I were encouraged to learn instruments. In Tony's case, instruments in the plural turned out to be true, beginning with the piano. The piano, together with the radiogram, three-piece suite, bookcase and display cabinet containing the best and never used crockery, made up the full complement of our front room furniture. From the piano, Tony worked his way through a collection of instruments including viola, guitar and tuba, finally settling on the euphonium. To this day he still expresses himself on the euphonium as an amateur musician with great diligence.

Tony and his wife retired to France several years ago after a lifetime in teaching and his continually active retirement, (ignoring his nodding off in front of the television at the end of the day) is spent keeping several acres of land under control, building sheds, indulging in numerous recreational activities and operating a *gite* for half the year. He also finds time to play his euphonium in his local village band, Harmonie, as well as in an altogether grander and more proficient wind band in Cahors; both groups requiring weekly rehearsals and personal practice.

On arrival in the suburbs of London at the age of five, I attended Park Lane Primary School in the borough of Romford, which is where I had my first violin lesson. This didn't happen immediately, the opportunity arising four years later when I was nine.

It was the policy of the local education authority that during the last two years of primary school, Wednesday afternoons were given over to various forms of creativity. Pupils were presented with a choice of activities, such as basketwork, painting, etc. The choice was left entirely up to the pupil and, once made, was pursued for the following two years.

Peter Allsop, my best mate at school, was familiarly known as Tad (Tad was short for Tadpole as his older brother's soubriquet was frog, because he looked like a frog). Tad and I were rascals: we sat at the back of the classroom and consistently behaved badly and when it came to making our Wednesday afternoon choices, the only benchmark that occurred to us, was which activity appears the silliest. Learning the violin won hands-down.

It's possible all thirty children in the class thought playing the violin was the silliest option, but we were the only two prepared to allow the element of perversity dictate our choice. The school now had two violinists in the making and our parents were delighted at the maturity and wisdom of the choices made by their nine-year-old sons. Little did they know of our reason and little did they realise how much this decision would determine the course of the rest of their sons' lives.

Tad and I had a joint lesson once a week and it soon became apparent that we both had an aptitude for the violin. Added to this unexpected development, we were even more surprised to discover we enjoyed the entire learning process. Daily practice did necessitate a degree of cajoling, but we succumbed and managed to follow a much-encouraged regimen without too much hardship – and made rapid progress.

Incentive to practice came from the challenge of acquiring violin technique and not from the more romantic notion of a love of music, although three pieces from those first two years of lessons from Helen Matthews made a strong musical impression.

Being able to perform an arrangement of a familiar piece reasonably well was extremely rewarding and with the lyrical folksong 'Greensleeves', I was able to achieve this for the first time. At the other extreme, an Allegro by Joseph Fiocco was memorable for getting my fingers and bowing arm working furiously through an entire piece in a series of near continuous semiquavers. The only other piece I can recall with any clarity and affection was my first concerto, a beginner's work by Leo Portnoff.

Up to this point my only involvement in music had come through membership of a church choir which did nothing to stimulate any latent musical or pious propensities I might have had. Before the advent of television in our house, all entertainment – with the exception of seasonal visits to circus and pantomime and Saturday morning cinema – was via the wireless.

The wireless set itself was a source of entertainment, from the high-pitched squeals that emerged when trying to locate a station or wavelength to trying to avoid electrocution when tweaking the valves round the back of the set. I remember with great affection how the whole family gathered weekly to listen to The Goon Show. I would always prop myself on the arm of the large leather armchair closest to the wireless so as not to miss a single word of a show that was mostly conceived and written by the funniest man that ever lived, Spike Milligan.

Unfortunately learning the violin did nothing to curb my rebellious streak and inevitably before too long an incident takes place which leads to my parents being summoned to the school with me in tow. In the Headmistress' study, Miss Paget recounts the drama to my parents with a severe warning, stating that a similar incident in the future would have more

Author aged 17, Hornchurch

profound consequences. The severe reprimand is accompanied by removal of my sub-prefect status and instructions to apologise to both violin teacher and headmistress. I clearly remember the reason for saying 'Fuck Off' to Helen Matthews, the kindly, competent and elderly violin teacher; it was out of sheer bravado. I was not in the least bit angry, I had just dared myself and was more than likely looking for a tad of Tad approbation at the same time.

After primary school, Tad and I went our separate ways but kept in touch. After secondary school, Tad attended the Birmingham School of Music followed by a stint at Oxford University, carving out an academic career in music, culminating in the post of Professor of Music at Exeter University.

I have much to thank Helen Matthews for, not least for her continuing faith in me through her forgiving and wise tutelage and successfully putting me forward at the end of my time at primary school for a scholarship to the Guildhall School of Music and Drama (GSM&D) as a Junior Exhibitioner. The scholarship ran simultaneously with my secondary school years and entailed travelling by tube to Blackfriars in the city of London every Saturday morning.

There, I was provided with four hours of free music tuition, alongside many other children from all over the home counties who had also been fortunate enough to have gained similar scholarships. I did this for the six years of my secondary school education before going full-time at GSM&D in 1963.

One downside to this arrangement was that Saturdays were also the time when interschool sporting competitions took place and as I was just as keen on sport as music, this meant I rarely got the chance to play for the school rugby and cricket teams, both of which I was a member. Occasionally the term times of the respective institutions didn't quite coincide and I could snatch the odd game.

My secondary school education took place at Coopers' Company School in Mile End, which created another downside to my educational provision. For the next six years, I had to spend two hours daily, six days a week wasting my life away on the District Line. I sometimes injected interest by experimenting with different routes. The most diverting one entailed travelling in the opposite direction to begin with, from Upminster Bridge to Upminster, then transferring to a steam train coming from Southend, finally arriving at the terminus at Fenchurch Street. A short walk to Tower Hill got me back once more on the District Line for the last lap to Mile End. I'm not sure why I've detailed the journey in that direction, because I only ever did it in the opposite direction on my way home from school.

In retrospect, the journey was made all the more interesting in knowing that four years later, the Fenchurch Street to Southend Line would have witnessed the last gasps of steam locomotion.

Apart from sport at school, I am a less than diligent pupil. My six years pass, swinging from one extreme to the other. My rebellious nature is now obviously an integral facet of my personality and regularly manifests itself through secondary school as it did through primary school. One moment I'm in the Headmaster's study, staring at the linoleum floor as a prelude to receiving three-of-the-best from his dreaded cane, the next, I'm standing in front of the whole school in the assembly hall, playing *Jesu, joy of man's desiring*.

I reckon I made my decision to make violin playing my profession around the age of thirteen. The motivation came from a number of sources, but I think the most influential was from the pleasure and reward I derived from membership of the Essex Youth Orchestra.

There is a wonderful British tradition comprising a national network of county youth orchestras of which the EYO was one of the best. It wasn't only making music under the direction of some of the finest musicians in London that made it such an unforgettable experience. It was also by doing exactly what I liked doing more than anything else, in the company of so many like-minded people at such an impressionable and receptive age that made it a unique journey of discovery.

I lived for the school holidays, knowing another EYO course lasting a week or so, was on its way. I remained a member for eight years, counting every moment spent on these courses – each year finished with a tour, often abroad – as the happiest time of my life. Maybe the long-lasting euphoria in the EYO was due to the contrast to term time at school.

My excuse for being a complete academic failure at school was that I'd already decided to be a professional violinist. School work became an irrelevance and I did as little as possible to get by. My homework would be hastily completed on the tube with no attention to producing anything other than the basic requirement: not the most enlightened view of what the benefits of a well-rounded education could mean.

I loved playing the violin, but the music that was making the biggest impression on me was not coming from the world of classical music, not yet. The first piece that really got home to me was at the age of thirteen on an EYO course in the small town of Thaxted. We were playing billiards in the recreation room at the end of a rehearsal day and someone put on a record of either Fats Waller or Louis Armstrong, singing 'Ain't Misbehavin'' and it just seemed to align all my emotions, making me feel content and very happy.

When, by my early teens, my father finally relented on having a television in the house (rented only) having considered it morally corrupt and a thorough waste of time. Unlike our experience of the radio (closely curated by You-Know-Who) TV was eclectic, embracing all genres of music at a time when the pop music world was being turned upside down with the advent of Elvis Presley, the Beatles and many more. Popular music was now sneaking into the house on the TV: Kenny Ball with 'Midnight in Moscow' and The Temperance Seven's 'You're Driving Me Crazy' and 'Pasadena' and as the decade progressed, the long-term influence of the Kinks and the Rolling Stones made a great impression. This music lived happily beside the classical repertoire I was now getting to know intimately in the EYO: Sibelius' 2nd Symphony, Dvorak's 7th symphony, Manuel de Falla's Three Cornered Hat and Copland's Rodeo Suite all making a huge impact.

At age seventeen, I left school and went full-time at GSM&D for three years and in my final year, I was invited to lead an amateur symphony orchestra called the Forest Philharmonic, based in Walthamstow. The orchestra met once a week through term time, with each term culminating in a concert. The conductor was Frank Shipway and Frank was barmy! He was fixated on Herbert von Karajan and unashamedly modelled himself on this self-styled demigod. He didn't look like Karajan but did try to emulate Karajan's image by always taking rehearsals with a bulky white towel draped around his neck. His thick locks of jet-black hair were frequently flicked back ostentatiously and every bit of his conducting technique was carefully choreographed, from baton movements to the most striking setting of his head, profiles in particular. His behaviour and attitude were a pure caricature of Karajan and he came across as a rather frightening clown, making it hard to know if he intended to be humorous or not.

The printed programmes for each concert had the players' names listed by section as normal, but on closer inspection, it was obvious that the sections in reality were much smaller than the printed ones. The printed lists were obviously Frank's handiwork and were evidence that he did have a sense of humour albeit at a basic level, as they were peppered with fictitious German names and unlikely ones at that. As far as I was aware, Hans Pumpernickel, Walter Maktfahrt and Wilhelm Bumfelter were not members of the 1st violin section.

The conductor, Colin Davis, who Frank worked with as a repetiteur at Covent Garden, allegedly remarked of Frank, that he had the *Air de Grandeur*, but it wasn't accompanied by the required *Air de Knowledge* but instead, by the *Air de Bullshit*. For all the nonsense, I do remember my last concert being a wonderful experience. It included a riveting performance of 'Symphony Fantastique' by Berlioz.

Towards the end of an unremarkable three years at the

GSM&D, I felt the need to make some kind of mark and so, with other applicants I put myself forward to play Max Bruch's first violin concerto in G minor with the school's second orchestra in an end of term concert. Happily my application was successful and I gave a performance conducted by a post graduate student called Roy Wales. As good fortune would have it, Roy ran a student orchestra of his own and invited me to join his orchestra playing the Bruch on a little tour planned for the summer. This unexpected bonus started with a concert in the now demolished Commonwealth Institute building in London followed by one in Vevey, Switzerland, culminating in a final performance in The Dome of Les Invalides in Paris.

That summer continued to throw up the unexpected and I was faced with a predicament. I had been accepted by Max Rostal, the renowned Austrian born violin teacher, to continue my studies with him in Switzerland, but this was dependent on finding the money to fund it. Meantime, while the process of seeking the necessary financial support was underway, an alternative path suddenly presented itself.

During my final year at GSM&D, a group of friends from the Essex Youth Orchestra formed an ensemble. Bill Gordon, the 1st horn was the moving force behind the idea and I was more than grateful to accept his offer when asked to lead the group. We promoted several concerts in a variety of instrumentation, from quartets to octets and I found the experience a great confidence booster for whatever was to come in the summer, when we would all be going our separate ways.

As the summer holiday loomed, out of the blue came a

phone call from Bill. He told me that he had just been appointed 1st horn in the newly formed Ulster Orchestra and that it was still looking for players to fill some of the key positions. 'How do you fancy the job of Sub-Leader?' He had recommended me to Maurice Miles, the Principal conductor and the person responsible for forming this new orchestra, who was apparently interested in hearing me audition.

Funding my further studies in Switzerland was proving to be no easy task, so I decided I had nothing to lose by auditioning and could always, in the unlikely event of being offered the job, turn it down. I auditioned with little expectation of success considering I was only twenty and had no professional experience. To my great surprise, I was offered the job.

Fairly quickly, I decided that such an opportunity at the beginning of my career was too portentous to let pass and accepted with a great deal of excitement tinged with a degree of trepidation at the responsibility that would now lie ahead.

Any regrets at not continuing my studies with Max Rostal were slightly offset by reminding myself of a display of ruthlessness I had witnessed at one of Rostal's masterclasses in London. (The two teachers of the Rostal method at GSM&D, Joan Spencer – my teacher – and Nannie Jamieson encouraged all their students to take part in these yearly masterclasses.)

Philip Clarke had just performed a movement of Walton's viola concerto which was received with exceptional praise by Rostal, opening his critique with, 'I don't know what to say' and going on to suggest during a substantial lesson that he should have six months playing the violin as a means of getting to grips with a more technically demanding repertoire that is not available on the viola.

Philip was followed by a mature student, married with a family and paying his way through the performer's course. A movement of Tchaikovsky's violin concerto was Charles Beldom's chosen work, on conclusion of which Rostal once again opened his criticism with, 'I don't know what to say'.

Rostal then offered, after a lengthy theatrical pause, the withering comment, 'Give it up before it's too late.'

Towards the end of the sixties I bumped into Charles in Withers famous violin shop in Wardour Street, Soho, a shop that no longer exists. Ignoring Rostal's less than encouraging words, he had continued playing and was at that time leading 2nd violins in the orchestra for what was then London Festival Ballet.

Incidentally, I was in Withers in search of a bow and was told by the assistant, as we stood separated by a large glass topped counter under which dozens of bows were on display, that they had none for sale. Looking down at the plenitude of bows staring up at me, I said 'What are all these doing here then?"

He simply answered, 'Making money'.

THREE

Embarking on a professional career presents steeper and broader learning curves, musical and domestic. 'What does a vacuum cleaner look like?'

It's August 1966, the Ulster Orchestra, a chamber orchestra of thirty players was about to take off. Bill and I decided to travel to Belfast by car rather than plane, giving us the option to transport more of our personal stuff. Neither of us owned a vehicle so Bill borrowed his father's capacious Austin Westminster and we set off for Stranraer and the ferry to Belfast. We had already taken out a year's lease on a Victorian terraced house on Donegal Road, close to Sandy Row and the city centre. We were sharing this three-bedroom mansion (the largest house I'd ever lived in) with another close friend from the Essex Youth Orchestra, 2nd trumpet Peter Cameron.

The house was more than sufficient for our needs, but it didn't take us long to put our stamp on the space, by reducing it to something more resembling an abandoned squat. All three of us were living away from our parents for the first time and celebrated the lack of authoritarianism hovering over us, by freeing ourselves from the shackles of tidiness. Our total disregard for everything our parents had ever attempted to school us in spread into every corner of the house like an invading virus, even though we owned the most meagre of belongings. We were yet to realise the benefits of maintaining a certain degree of neatness in order to avoid the attendant frustrations, with Bill receiving the most plaudits as the most slovenly by far.

We took turns cooking the evening meal. Peter and I were only capable of producing the worst of staple student cuisine, from Vesta curries to congealed spaghetti Bolognese, whereas Bill was altogether more adventurous, producing meals which might include such delicacies as crepe suzettes, with maybe flambé tea towel as a side dish, as he consistently and effortlessly transformed the kitchen into a Health Inspector's nightmare. Even so, Bill's meals were always the best.

Of the three bedrooms, Bill had managed to bag the main one at the front of the house. Peter and I were perfectly happy with this arrangement; after all, Bill had been responsible for finding the property. This room was spacious with a couple of sash cord windows overlooking Donegal Road. Bill spent a lot of time in this room, often at hours not normally reserved for sleeping, as he was plagued by an extraordinary sleep disorder, a disorder that was not medically recognised, nor was it a serious health issue in the usual run of things; it wouldn't have even been classified as debilitating if there happened to have been twenty-six hours in a day. His bedroom was in a permanent state of disarray. Drawers were ignored in preference for the floor, wardrobe and coat hangers made redundant. When it came to household dust, he was so fearless, he never discovered the vacuum cleaner and that dusters are yellow.

Bill habitually went to bed late, which became progressively later each day and eventually over a two to three-week period, a complete night vanished, He then slept through the following day and night, waking very early the next morning. This completed his cycle, allowing him to begin all over again.

During one of these extended slumbers, it struck Peter and I, that it might be amusing to interrupt the comatose Bill in mid repose. On our chosen afternoon, we slunk silently into Bill's room, checked that he was sound asleep and once confirmed, we opened the curtains and raised as quietly as possible, the two sash cord windows facing his bed. We then retreated, shutting the door behind us. Bill slept on.

We then made for the street, armed with a dozen fresh eggs each. From there, we laid siege to his room lobbing our nutritious missiles through his open windows. How the moment of awaking hit Bill we could only guess, but his first reaction was impossible to miss. The expletives penetrated through the traffic noise of busy Donegal Road; it was our signal to retreat and rapidly disappear from the scene.

It wasn't long before we had to face and pacify an angry horn player and confront the result of our mischief. The episode had badly backfired, as it quickly dawned on us that Bill's newly decorated bedroom would have to be returned to its original state – by me and Peter. The cleaning of the organic yolk and albumen wallpaper looked like a daunting task, although certainly worthy of a contemporary art prize. The rest of the room looked even more of a challenge, with clothes, carpet and bedlinen looking like preparations for a giant Spanish omelette.

After the incident, our relationship soon settled back to how it was before. All was forgiven and Bill resumed his eccentric sleeping pattern. Unfortunately, this recurring pattern didn't fit well with the regularity of the orchestra's schedule and the incompatibility was now compromising his health, which in turn was affecting the quality of his playing.

This was the beginning of our professional careers and an immensely challenging time. Not only were the three of us trying to learn new skills of a domestic nature, but fresh from music college, we had an even greater task in learning a whole new raft of pieces written for chamber orchestra. At my college, five hours per week were devoted to learning the symphony orchestra repertoire with only two hours allocated to that of a chamber orchestra. I'm sure this was typical of all colleges at the time and that for the many recently graduated players of the Ulster Orchestra (UO) limited exposure to the chamber orchestra repertoire meant that every week, a handful of unknown works had to be mastered and performed to a professional standard. The Serenade for Strings by Dvorak and the Holberg Suite by Grieg were revelations. The lush and deeply moving timbre achieved by a strings-only ensemble made an everlasting mark on me.

In the first few weeks of rehearsals, as members of the

orchestra adapted to their roles and each other, a number of changes of position were made. In my case, my lack of maturity and professional experience caught up with me and rather undermined my confidence resulting in reassignment as principal 2nd, a role with a lesser degree of responsibility.

Part of my learning process as a principal player included bowing the sections' parts. This involved marking the direction of the bow over certain notes to fit with similar passages, usually in the 1st violins, or to complement the flow or dynamic demands of the music and sometimes to fulfil a request by the conductor. This all done swiftly and unobtrusively.

Although Bill didn't have the encumbrance of bowings to contend with, he did have a conspicuous solo line to play. Most of the time Bill performed wonderfully, playing with great musicality, a beautiful tone and bags of personality. The demands made on a 1st horn in an orchestra are so great, that technical security is a must at all times and in Bill's case this was not happening. His unreliable playing became a matter of grave concern and the unavoidable happened: he was replaced as the orchestra's inaugural year came to a close.

In many ways Bill fell on his feet soon after. He moved to Manitoba in Canada and almost immediately found an opening as lecturer and horn teacher in the music department at Brandon University. This, combined with freelancing with the Winnipeg Symphony Orchestra, gave him a secure and varied existence and in time he became Dean of the Music Department with a regular slot presenting an Arts programme on the local TV station. Fifty years later, he is still teaching and playing in Brandon and recently diversified into conducting, presently holding the post of Principal conductor of a community symphony orchestra in Winnipeg.

I should mention in answer to that oft-asked question of musicians, 'What made you take up your particular instrument?' Bill's answer is as unromantic as mine, though his reasoning contains a little more sagacity. He had an accident as a child, puncturing one of his lungs and the surgeon who put him back together advised him to take up the French horn to strengthen his one remaining lung. So, he did.*

---

*Sadly, in the time since writing this chapter, Bill has died quite peacefully, and presumably, sleeping undisturbed.

FOUR

Sorry to disappoint but orchestral life has got a lot more boring in the 21st century. 'By the way, how do you like your eggs?'

A few days short of my twenty-first birthday, my virginity was cunningly removed by a principal player in the orchestra. I had resolved in my teens to stay celibate until the age of twenty-one. By then I expected to be mature enough to appreciate the full weight of graduating to that significant stage of growing up (crude, boastful claims from certain members of my peer group and my father's moral values weighing heavily on this decision). I thought I had done pretty well to get that far and was not too bothered at succumbing a couple of days early.

The prelude to our coupling was food; it was seduction by scrambled eggs. The most mouth-watering scrambled eggs I had ever tasted. Cooked in butter, folded rather than scrambled and with no added milk, (my mother would add milk, a habit left over from war time rationing to make the food go further) leaving me unable to say no.

The 2nd oboe, David Thomas was one of the first to leave the orchestra. Dave was thirty, an oddball and very well liked. His dark tousled hair, John Lennon spectacles before they became fashionable, ill-fitting clothes and a curious ever-present smile along with his oboe and case gave the distinct impression everything was home-made.

His car was indeed home-made and not from a kit. It was cobbled together from the second-hand parts of scrapped cars, with new parts utilised when essential. Its style was that of a two-seater, open-top tourer, but that is a far too flattering description for something that more accurately resembled a gigantic, motorised Meccano set on wheels. Despite its rudimentary build, Dave, with constant tinkering used it on a daily basis. Dave's pastures new were going to be New Zealand and given the manner of his departure, the other side of the world was undoubtedly an excellent choice. There was a British orchestral tradition that a departing member celebrated their leaving, by having a drink or two on the day of their final performance, a tradition strongly encouraged by colleagues. Dave's farewell performance was no exception and took place in the Ulster Hall, Belfast's main concert hall.

The Ulster Hall is built in the traditional nineteenth century oblong shape, with a high stage sloping gently from back to front and the piece to be performed is Handel's Messiah. The Messiah is scored for strings, oboes, bassoon, trumpets, (or *thrumpets* as in Maurice Miles' gentrified perversion of the orthodox pronunciation) timpani and harpsichord so it's a comparatively small group. In addition to the orchestra there are four solo singers, who usually occupy the front of the stage and a chorus positioned at the back of the stage. The orchestra is cosily sandwiched between the two. As the orchestra contains no heavyweights in the form of trombones, French horns, or percussion, sections that normally sit at the rear of the orchestra, the woodwind section now finds itself occupying that position instead, sitting directly in front of the chorus who are literally breathing down their necks.

Dave, true to tradition has conscientiously downed a liberal number of pints by the time he arrives for the evening performance, though outwardly there is little evidence of the vast amount of beer contained in his average-sized frame.

The performance begins and Dave plays in time, in tune and at the correct volume. But, in his present condition, the heroic effort of concentration needed to keep control is disproportionately assigned to these tasks and his inability to adequately apportion attention to other parts of his body, including a busily active diaphragm in close proximity to his over challenged bladder, means something is going to lose out. Unfortunately, halfway through the first half of the concert, the concentration diverted to his lower regions lapses and control of his bladder is suddenly lost.

The flood gates now open and closing them is not an option. The initial trickle soon turns into a stream, lapping its way through the orchestra to the front of the gently raked stage. Dave plays on like a true professional. The front row of the chorus is horrified at what is taking place right under their noses and they too are forced to make special efforts of concentration as their olfactory senses come in for a battering.

For the rest of us, another form of control needs our

attention. Giggling in an orchestra can be as infectious as an outbreak of German measles in a Bavarian children's hospital and it's now threatening to completely disrupt the performance: the insidious nature of giggling is quite capable of wiping out whole segments of an orchestra.

Somehow, after withstanding the deluge of stimulation, the interval arrives at its assigned moment, with the performance still intact. There is a lot of muttering back-stage, quite a lot of laughter and a few minor recriminations. Amazingly, Dave reappears for the second half, slightly damper than when the evening began and the performance is completed with no further incident. Overall, the audience was oblivious to the additional entertainment that has just played out.

Dave departs for New Zealand the next day in his overloaded motorised Meccano set, happy in the knowledge that his farewell, of mythical proportions has lived up to the orchestra's expectations and a chorus of *Safe journey Dave* from a representative coterie of admirers sees him off. A prayer to St. Christopher could have appeared a mite too hypocritical and carried little weight in assisting his forthcoming journey, considering his unorthodox interpretation of religious devotion the previous evening.

Orchestral life has got a lot more boring. Dave's episode would be unlikely to happen in the present funding climate as the risk of losing sponsorship is a major preoccupation for most managements, with orchestras employing whole departments devoted to raising cash from sponsors. Players are only too aware of the serious repercussions that might arise from a misdemeanour on the scale of David's and generally behave with the expected decorum. I suppose it just might be possible for someone to avoid instant dismissal were the same thing to happen today, if the orchestra's main sponsor happened to be a company responsible for the manufacture of medication for the relief of prostatitis. . .

FIVE

In building camaraderie in a fledgling orchestra, members need to learn to crawl before they learn to stagger. 'Is that Handel's Water Music I hear?'

At a guess the average age of the Ulster Orchestra at its foundation was around twenty-four or twenty-five, mainly due to the large group of players straight out of music colleges taking up their first jobs. A second group of players, had to be employed from amongst those already domiciled in Northern Ireland as a stipulation by the Northern Ireland Arts Council, the Orchestra's largest funding body.

Along with one or two unattached individuals making up the full complement, an influential third group hailed from Dublin, was slightly older and arrived with experience from the Radio Telefis Éireann Orchestra. It included three Hungarians who had fled Hungary during the 1956 Uprising, a Frenchman, a Sri Lankan and a handful of Irish nationals. From this group the leaders of four of the five string sections were appointed, giving the orchestra a solid base on which to build.

The solidity was to be relatively short-lived, as from this group of players, the foreign musicians saw an otherwise previously limited opportunity to eventually work in the rest of the United Kingdom, London in particular. It was not possible to work in England, Scotland and Wales, directly from the Republic of Ireland as a foreign national, but due to an anomaly in the legal structure of the UK and the Republic of Ireland, it was possible to work in Northern Ireland and once resident in the North for two years, one could legally work in the UK. London has always been one of the great music hubs of the world and so the opening up of this route was irresistible to the ambitious, making the two-year hiatus just a minor frustration – any impatience at having to wait the course was well offset by being in at the birth of a new orchestra with all the attendant attractions.

The first few weeks of rehearsals were devoted to familiarising ourselves with the works which would form the backbone of the UO's basic repertoire.

The overtures of Rossini and Mozart produced staple fare with Rossini's Silken Ladder giving Tessa the 1st oboe another challenge in the inaugural concert which she once again successfully negotiated. The enormous symphonic outpouring from Haydn and Mozart provided essential fillings alongside the symphonies of Schubert and discovering Prokofiev's Classical Symphony and Bizet's symphony in C were wonderful revelations for me. But there were other less laudable things to learn.

Organisations employing large numbers of people – the military, universities and so forth – develop bonding rituals and traditions in the course of their formation, which help to establish and secure their futures. The same applies to orchestras.

In 1967, the UO attempted to initiate its first tradition and deferred to the greater experience of the Dublin clique for guidance. Today we are more health conscious in our choice of group activities: a day out on bicycles or a regular Pilates class; in 1967, health considerations were nowhere in evidence. Brian, our Principal viola was the man entrusted with choice and organisation of our first *tradition*, the universal pub-crawl. He was no stranger to a pint of Guinness and participation in the occasional pub-crawl, so everyone had great faith and high expectations that a successful day would be in the offing.

Brian drew up a set of simple pub-crawl rules, simple but definitely challenging: twelve pubs, designated in advance and the consumption of a pint of beer, Guinness, or lager in the space of half-an-hour in each pub. The pubs he picked were so close together that no travel time needed to be wasted in the six-hour-long schedule. A suitable day was chosen, with an early lunchtime start.

The number of participants at the outset was reasonable, with the expectation that those with a modicum of good sense at knowing their own limitations would join later, while others would peel off as they reached saturation point. Some like me, incapable of sinking anything like the required quantity of beer, anticipated doing both, joining late and departing early leaving the original hard core of committed devotees to attempt the challenge in its entirety.

The crawl was going well as it reached the halfway mark with everyone coping with the pace. The crawlers were by and large behaving responsibly with just a suggestion of raucousness beginning to creep in. As we entered pub number eight, we found the bar staff much less welcoming than in earlier establishments: by now it was very apparent that we are exuding a good deal more than mere joviality. In truth, we were becoming rather boisterous, slightly off balance in some cases and giving off an air of something barely contained lurking just below the surface, rather like the first hesitant hisses from the spout of a whistling kettle.

We were served, albeit grudgingly; we downed our pints and departed, leaving behind a slightly damp floor from a small amount of spillage. I was now replete and decided to abandon the project and head home, even though I hadn't started at the beginning and had only consumed a pathetic five pints. The schedule was still intact with no major incidents to report and I left the remaining effervescent devotees to continue to the next watering hole.

Details surrounding the remainder of the crawl emerged later. News came through that the crawl didn't manage to reach completion, having been brought to a halt by the inability of certain dedicated party members to negotiate an accident-free passage to the lavatory. This dwindling group, some of whom had wet themselves while still standing at the bar, was ejected from pub number whatever, bringing the day's valiant efforts to an abrupt close.

However, Brian was reluctant to let go the idea of establishing a pub crawl on the orchestra's social itinerary, simply because of one aborted attempt. With commendable tenacity, a few days later, having reviewed the strategy, he came up with a cunning plan that he thought should ensure success on a second attempt and organised another foray. The rules were the same but with one important innovation, a dress code. Brian had a theory that society perceives and judges each one of us by our appearance to such an extent that, however unacceptable our behaviour, short of violence, it will be tolerated if we are attired in a manner commensurate with a certain image.

It worked. A couple of weeks later, the crawl comported itself in behaviour that was no better than on the first outing, but notwithstanding, managed to run its full course and the first Ulster Orchestra tradition was established, becoming a yearly event. An addendum was then added to the pub-crawl rules making it mandatory that all those taking part were to be dressed in concert clothes consisting of a full set of tails, including waistcoat and bow-tie – a code for female crawlers had yet to be decided.

I might be giving the impression that life in the Ulster Orchestra revolved around the condition of the male bladder. It's not altogether true, there were variations on the theme.

Another tradition established early on, was the New Year's Eve party. The first was given by János, one of the Hungarian contingent and Leader of the Orchestra. Importantly, it was an open house for the whole orchestra, with the only incident of any consequence occurring when János mysteriously disappeared about ten-thirty, which as host of a New Year's Eve party seemed a mite strange. His wife, Antoinette wasn't unduly concerned, as she knew but didn't let on what the rest of us didn't know. János had imbibed a little too much on an empty stomach and had vomited down the lavatory. During this expulsion, the contents of his stomach had attached themselves to a denture holding his two front teeth and before realising it, János had flushed the lot down the pan. Too vain to reappear with a gaping void where his teeth would have normally been, he took himself off to bed.

The following two years saw the New Year party tradition firmly established, with an open house policy fundamental to its existence. But in the fourth year, there was an unpopular departure from the norm.

A relatively new member had offered to host the party. Paul was our twenty-two-year-old, sub-principal bass and shared a flat with John, a prominent member of the N.I. Arts Council. Between them, they were throwing that year's party, but with one glaring difference: it wasn't an open house. It was by invitation only and the guest list appeared to only include those of a certain standing in the community: Head of the Arts Council, Principal conductor, Professors, Composers, Councillors etc. This didn't sit comfortably with the egalitarian ideals of the orchestra, who in almost complete number was now gathered on New Year's Eve at the Windsor Tennis Club: the company was well aware that the assembled 'dignitaries' were only a couple of streets away.

The Windsor tennis club was a good place to know when your working day often finished after ten-o-clock at night, a time coinciding with what was then pub closing time. The tennis club had a private drinking licence, allowing drinking outside the normal licensing hours for members and their guests; seemingly unlimited numbers of guests as I think only two people in the orchestra were members and it quickly had become a regular haunt for the orchestra.

We congregate this New Year's Eve in small clusters drowning our sorrows, with Paul and John's party unavoidably the big talking point. I'm in a group which included Brian and his constant companion, a cellist called Marjorie, the owner of a vintage 'R' type Bentley. Brian is an impressive looking character, tall with military bearing and sporting a wonderfully voluminous grey moustache which cascades from under his nose, obscuring his top lip. This impressive moustache is the object of much self-pampering, exemplified when being dexterously parted by thumb and index finger of Brian's left hand, in preparedness to supping from his frequent glasses of Guinness. Brian is fuming over Paul and John's lack of social awareness.

It's now getting close to midnight and revenge on the hosts of the exclusive New Year party is being contemplated. 'Do you know what I would like to do?' quizzes Brian. Not waiting for an answer, he quickly volunteers, 'I'd like to go round there and shit on their doorstep.' None of us is in a frame of mind to disabuse him of the idea and after a few moments of cogitation, he bellows, 'Marjorie, go and fetch the Bentley.' (Brian doesn't drive and relies on Marjorie as chauffeur much of the time.)

The three of us drive the short distance to Eglantine Avenue and park outside the main door flat. It has a small, tiled entrance hall between an inner front door and a more substantial door to the street. This outer door is frequently left ajar in these type of properties as in this case, giving a more welcoming feel to anyone arriving, which considering what is about to happen seems a little ironic.

Being close to midnight the party is well underway and more guests are unlikely to arrive and we are even more certain none will leave before the old year is out. Marjorie is spared witnessing the iniquity which is about to unfold and is left behind the wheel of the getaway vehicle while Brian and I move stealthily through the open outer door, closing it behind us. We can hear a gentle burble of voices coming from behind the inner door, as Brian loses no time in divesting himself of his lower garments, expertly balancing himself in a squatting position and delivering a perfectly crafted turd to the tiled floor, accompanied by an appropriate amount of urine. He then returns himself to a state of sartorial elegance, reaches into his trouser pocket and produces a lipstick which he had previously liberated from Marjorie's handbag. With this, he writes in clear, bold letters on the wallpaper, *HAPPY NEW YEAR FROM THE ULSTER ORCHESTRA*.

Revenge now satisfied, we leave, fully shutting the outer door behind us, thereby trapping Brian's offering in a small unventilated space, awaiting the departure of the poor unsuspecting guests.

I can't help marvelling at Brian's ability to conjure up ordure at will as we return to the tennis club to a hero's welcome and a much-improved mood: the reason for our sudden departure having filtered through to the rest of the assemblage in our absence.

The rest of the New Year is celebrated with great levity, especially when detail of the mission is elaborated upon and an extra underlying sense of excitement is generated by wondering what the result of our prank will be.

A few days later, we had our first rehearsal of 1970 and expected to be faced with recriminations and possible retribution, but nothing happened, absolutely nothing. The incident was never mentioned by Paul and for obvious reasons we never broached the subject.

Paul left the Ulster Orchestra later that year and it became obvious in the years following that the incident had left no stain on his character. He went on to have an illustrious career as Principal Bass in the Scottish National Orchestra, Co-principal in the London Symphony Orchestra and spent twenty years as Principal in the BBC Symphony Orchestra.

To this day, I have no idea what transpired when that inner door on Eglantine Avenue was opened in the early hours of January 1st, 1970. Paul died in 2019, so I probably never will.

SIX

An outdated Gauloises Orchestral Technique for string players explained. 'Beware, it carries a health warning.'

At the age of fifteen, I joined the fraternity of smokers. I passed the initiation test with flying colours having sensed only the merest hint of nausea when inhaling my first few drags on my first cigarette.

Image. I was searching for an image which would show to the world my sophistication and intellectual maturity and smoking was the obvious building block. Unlike today, smoking was associated with glamour, artistry and success: Camus, Sartre, Picasso and Ravel were all avid smokers, Gauloise Disque Bleu being their cigarette of choice. The industry's promotional tone was, *nothing but good things come from this little tube of pure delight.*

To add further to my image, I adopted a slight stoop when walking and carried my music satchel tucked under one arm rather than use the odd but perfectly serviceable handle. A final tweak came by adorning my neck with a Paisley-patterned cravat. It half crossed my mind to add an academic stutter, *if you know w-w-what I mean,* but thank goodness, a modicum of realism intervened and I resisted.

Even without the stutter, this pretentious stratagem was pathetic in the extreme, managing to achieve the exact opposite of what was intended and was discarded before you could say *Harold Wilson's pipe.* However, in the twinkling of an eye the smoking had become full-blown addiction which would last for twenty years.

As a deterrent to action, recourse to the comfort of smoking was highly effective, allowing me to regularly put off anything that I really didn't want to face. I hadn't fully realised the magnitude of this phenomenon on my everyday life until the day I gave up. The benefit to my health was one obvious plus from quitting smoking, but the secondary unexpected benefit, my willingness now to face reality, was equally profound. Smoking was immediately elevated to the top of my list of regrets and remains so to this day. Tobacco companies, advertising agencies and complicit governments around the world have a lot to answer for, stretching over several decades. They have been responsible for churning out massive amounts of knowingly misleading propaganda that has resulted in millions of unnecessary deaths, with accountability nowhere to be seen. Real power lies with those who control minds.

The four years I spend in Belfast were four of my smoking years and smoking controlled my life to a great extent. I was so dedicated to the habit, that the moment I woke in the morning, I would lean out of bed in search of my packet of fags. This had been strategically positioned within arm's length on the floor next to an ashtray just under the bed and I would light up before registering complete consciousness. I kept going on twenty-a day until retiring for the night and took my last puff in bed before switching out the light.

A goodly number of my colleagues and visiting conductors were equally addicted. Unbelievably, we smoked during rehearsals, so a useful bit of additional violin technique, specifically aimed at the smoking violinist/violist had to be learnt: clasping lightly the end of the cigarette furthest from the ignited end, between the base of first and second fingers of the bowing arm, it's possible to use the bowing arm in normal fashion, with little or no impediment to right arm technique. One exception occurs when pizzicato is required. . .

Believe it or not, we also smoked in theatre pits during opera rehearsals, dropping ash and stubbing out the dog-ends directly on the floor: the expression 'passive smoking' was yet to be coined.

As the staple repertoire of the orchestra was based on the inventive and ground-breaking symphonies of Joseph Haydn, Ludwig van Beethoven, prolific Wolfgang Amadeus Mozart and precocious Franz Schubert, it will come as no surprise to know that every one of the symphonies we played by these composers touched me greatly. Except for those of Mozart.

For me, Mozart's compositions fall into two categories, either hitting the right spot or failing to go very deep below the surface. It's as though writing only for certain combinations of instruments inspired him to produce true works of genius. It may sound outlandish that as a violinist and chamber musician and much as I enjoyed playing them, I lump together in the same category as the symphonies, the violin concertos and the string quartets. If nothing else, it suggests on my part a degree of impartiality.

The remaining output of Mozart that I'm familiar with, I find astounding in its emotional and technical content: piano concertos, operas, Sinfonia Concertante for violin and viola, viola quintets and the monumental Requiem.

The orchestra's repertoire each year also included a short season of opera. One particular year stood out in this regard and not for any musical reason. Antonio de Almeida was a conductor based in Paris, but for one week in 1967, he was based in Belfast. He had hired the entire orchestra, plus soloists and chorus for three performances in the Grand Opera House. It was a fairly unusual situation for a conductor to hire an opera production team and not the other way round and probably happens for one of only two reasons. Either the work to be performed is being championed by the conductor because no organisation is interested in that particular composition, or the conductor is thought not to be sufficiently competent for a company to engage them and the opportunity to conduct a professional opera perform-ance is only made possible if the whole thing is put on at their own expense.

Antonio's background was one of privilege and not being short of a bob or two, he fell firmly into the second category, allowing him to fulfil his ambition by circumventing the normal requirements demanded of most conductors. This was apparent right from the start; it was quite obvious that he had not mastered the necessary skills to successfully guide an opera production from first rehearsal through to final performance. His chosen opera was in fact an operetta, La Grande Duchesse de Gerolstein by Jacques Offenbach and by the third day of rehearsals the maestro's virtuosic failings had become a focal point and something was going to have to give. The scant respect we had for the job he was doing was now turning from boredom and frustration to that of antagonism as the orchestra came close to a state of hysteria. The players' behaviour degenerated, triggering an unedifying incident and the rest of the day dramatically altered.

As usual, the smokers had been conscientiously devoting themselves to their habit during the three days of rehearsals and the pit floor was beginning to resemble a large ashtray. Shuffling the growing mound of spent matches and dogends on the floor, started out as a distraction from the vexatious rehearsal, but soon transmogrified. Under the direction of the infamous Brian, also a smoker, (nothing but Gauloise Disque Bleu) the detritus was gathered up in a neat heap, right under the conductor's music stand, but out of his field of vision and with the help of a few sweet wrappers as kindling, set alight. Antonio was unaware of the incineration until the pungent fumes wafted above his stand, rudely interrupting proceedings. This was the final iniquity for a man already feeling under siege from his incalcitrant charges and an incredibly angry maestro finally lost his temper, stopped the rehearsal, fired off a tirade of invective and finished by accusing us of being unprofessional. At this point, Brian, who also happened to be the union representative leapt to his feet, saying, 'Whatever else you might call us, you cannot call us unprofessional, as by definition we are professionals because we're paid for our services.' He then added insult to injury by demanding an immediate apology.

Antonio in his present, furious state could hardly breathe let alone apologise and refused. Brian then says, 'We are not playing another note until you're prepared to stand in front of the whole orchestra, retract your accusation and assert that we *are* professionals.' Brian then led the orchestra out of the pit to await further developments.

Some two hours and a lost rehearsal later, the orchestra reassembled and the unfortunate man's humiliation was completed as he feigned ignominy, carried out the demands made upon him and apologised, retracting his accusation.

The week continued to its conclusion without further incident. The three performances took place without any major mishap despite the conductor and Antonio de Almeida's unceremonious departure was the last we ever saw of him.

However, without doubt this incident was a gross misuse of union power. Perhaps we perpetrators should have been expelled from the Musician's Union for as professionals we clearly demonstrated unprofessional behaviour. I've always understood the necessity for trade unions and organised labour – I was a union steward myself in the Northern Sinfonia – but my father's experience in the newspaper trade was a good example of non-acceptance of change and abuse of the system. As new technology was introduced, the small workforce of four or five men on his nightshift at Odhams Press soon realised that they could easily cope one person short on the Saturday night shift. They then took it in turns to take the Saturday shift off unbeknown to management. My father, the only one to find this deception deeply immoral felt he had no alternative but to go along with his colleagues as to have refused would have led to an intolerable work environment, as he was already constantly under strain from being seen as different. I'm afraid this kind of incident might even have made it easier for the rise and subsequent wrecking work of the Thatcher years.

SEVEN

Toys are all well and good, although certain adult toys are not everyone's cup of tea: 'If you can, try to resist wind-up conductors.'

The young and burden-free players of the Ulster Orchestra were about to join the consumer society. A world previously unavailable to most of us had suddenly, with regular income, come comfortably within reach and the spending could now begin.

The first indulgence was always going to be a car, especially now that distance from home had made borrowing mum and dad's car no longer possible and petrol at five shillings a gallon (six-and-a-half pence a litre) was very affordable. Most of my colleagues were only interested in owning new models whereas I had a hankering for something of an earlier vintage, a more adventurous choice of vehicle with romantic connotations. An older car also had the added attraction of being a lot cheaper and though flush with my newfound wealth, I was still trying to exert a degree of financial caution.

Theme and Variations

I wasn't investing in my first car. In my last couple of months as a student I had bought a 1946 Morris 10 which was constantly in need of repair. A poor investment and quickly despatched before it landed me in huge debt. In Belfast I chose a 1952 Sunbeam Talbot 90 as my second car. Unlike the Morris, this was in proper working order, or reasonably so and the first of five iconic models I owned over the next four years.

Although financial considerations played their part in my choices, the overriding reason for my selections was more to do with a deep-rooted affection for the toy cars I played with as a child. Firmly embedded fond memories of particular toys unconsciously surfaced at a time when they could be replaced by the real thing.

At Christmas 1948 I received a pedal car, but this was less stimulating as a car, more as a set of wheels akin to a scooter or bicycle. My first real interest in cars was brought about by my limited and treasured collection of Dinky Toys which took me into a world of inexhaustible make-believe. My clockwork train set (the family's income was insufficient for the luxury of owning an electric version) had the restrictions of its fixed, unexciting layout and couldn't match the world I was able to conjure up with the help of my Dinky Toys.

Besides one or two military vehicles, a couple of planes, a fire engine and a smattering of industrial and farm vehicles, it was the cars that fired my imagination most.

They were easily carried in my pocket and whenever the urge was upon me, I could simply and instantly fashion out a circuit in the garden, using soil and any furniture found in a typical garden. My cars flew, crashed unscathed (at worst,

Author's pedal car, Norwich, 1948

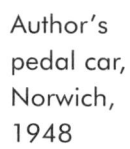

dislodging a tyre or chipping the paintwork) and were dropped and thrown in any number of imaginary situations. I remember vividly being captivated by three models in particular: a two-tone blue Ford Zephyr 6; a red Maserati racing car (I still have it); and a white MG TC. These three must have been the key to a memory-locking mechanism that was released on my arrival in Belfast.

The Sunbeam was not two-tone blue, or two-tone anything, just boringly black. However, the rest fitted nicely with other criteria and the unwitting link to my Dinky Toys. The Sunbeam was fast and sporty, with leather upholstery adding more than a hint of luxury and the pleasingly understated slipstreamed bodywork gave an appearance of comforting, feminine lines.

I enjoyed a year exploring Northern Ireland in my new car with only one reservation, an issue with its design. Well, to be fair, the real fault was only highlighted by the car's design, the fault lying squarely in the design of the human body, not the car. A visit to the beach with three male colleagues was the day this fault came painfully to my attention.

In the Sunbeam, the four of us headed to the beach at

Millisle on the County Down coast, intending to mostly loll about in the sun. We did find enough energy to kick a ball around, skim a few pebbles and smoke a cigarette or two and shortly before we left we thought a tournament of a more boisterous nature might be fun: *Fighting Giants*, a competition in which the contestants team up in pairs with the lighter of each pair sitting on the shoulders of the heavier. With the pairs facing each other, one giant tries to destabilise the rival giant by using simple physical force, with the victor toppling his opponent to the ground. Pretty innocuous stuff on the soft sand of a beach if, when overbalanced, the lower partner releases the legs of the upper partner and a natural dismount occurs during the collapse.

I was the top half with Bill as base of our giant. Very quickly we were vanquished, with the two of us earthbound. Either Bill was a novice to this pastime, or he had spotted an opportunity to exact revenge on the egg tossing incident of a few weeks before and continued to clasp my legs in a vice-like grip throughout the entire collapse. We hit the sand as a giant intact, with me taking the full force of our combined weight on one of my hands.

A dislocated left thumb is not a pretty sight and neither is it painless when locked at an additional forty-five-degree angle. We were nowhere near a hospital and had no idea where a local doctor might be found in this sparsely populated hamlet, so opted for what we did know which meant driving the twenty miles to Bangor hospital's A&E Department. We had decided on this course of action even though the driver was going to be me. It had to be me as my companions are either unable or unwilling to drive my car with its steering column mounted gear lever. I got little sympathy from my passengers and even less as they observed me wrestling with the gear lever. The sight of my thumb sticking out at a jocular angle provided great amusement.

Once at the hospital, because of the pain, I was unable to keep my hand motionless long enough for an x-ray to be taken, so the doctor changed tack and opted for an immediate manipulation (anaesthetics had yet to reach the wilds of County Down). The manipulation was brutal but quick and successful, with my wrist and most of my thumb soon incarcerated in plaster.

The really painful part was yet to happen as we began the fifteen-mile drive back to Belfast. Engaging the gears was normally a clenched fist operation, but with a defunct thumb, I now needed to position the gear lever in the crook of my thumb and the palm of my hand, causing my thumb to come into closer proximity with the dashboard than would be normal. Inevitably, every movement of the lever in the direction of the dashboard resulted in my traumatised rigid thumb colliding with the dashboard followed by shooting pain. I peppered the whole journey with my full collection of cusses, which I am happy to report drew a further barrage of ribbing and unsuppressed hilarity from my sympathetic, erstwhile friends.

Two days later my thumb was still just as painful and the tip of my thumb and fingers were turning dark purple. I made a short journey by foot, to Belfast City hospital, had the plaster removed and a new cast put in place. My hand hadn't finished swelling from the trauma of the accident when the original plaster was applied two days earlier, severely restricting the blood supply to my extremities once the hand had fully expanded. I could now look forward to six weeks paid leave.

For those of you reading this for whom cars offer no interest, please feel free to skip the next three or four pages.

After the Sunbeam, I transferred my affections to a 1946 MG TC, an open-top sports car offering a completely different experience: uncomfortable, tricky to control and slow. (Some of my acquaintances might suggest it mirrored my personality perfectly.) It was also great fun. Its most idiosyncratic feature was the fuel gauge; there wasn't one, well not as we usually understand it. The petrol tank was fitted externally to the rear of the car where a boot would normally be and resembled a suitcase, albeit one made of steel and attached to the car by metal straps. To discover how much fuel was in the tank, I had to park the car and retrieve a metre-long wooden ruler from behind the seats. The ruler was marked with numbered notches, indicating each gallon and was lowered into the tank to discover the petrol level (serving the same purpose as an oil dipstick still does today). This wasn't as inconvenient as it sounds. With a pragmatic approach, I soon got into the habit when stationary for a reasonable amount of time, of checking the tank, thus avoiding having to make specific stops for this purpose. I also became more aware of petrol consumption by closely monitoring the mileage undertaken, becoming a dab hand at knowing what to expect at what speeds and particular road conditions. I ran the MG for two years, eventually fancying a change to something with a little more punch and with a hard top.

The orchestra changed its programme weekly and a typical week involved three days of rehearsals, two or three out-of-

A Scottish camping holiday, 1968

town concerts and finished the week with a concert in Belfast on a Saturday night. Our mid-week concerts took us to all the major cities and large towns throughout Northern Ireland such as Armagh, Strabane, Enniskillen and Derry. On those days, we made our own travel arrangements in contrast to some orchestras which had coach travel provided. We viewed these days as an opportunity to put our cars through their paces on the uncrowded roads and motorways with their unregulated speed limits.

There were really only five protagonists in this potentially hazardous pursuit, as participation was defined by the type of vehicle to be exercised:

Chris – Mini cooper.
Peter – Mini cooper 'S'.
Eddie – Sunbeam Tiger.
Peter – MG ZA Magnette.
Myself – Jaguar XK 140, special edition.

The cars belonging to the two clarinettists and flautist

were new, or almost, but mine and trumpeter Peter's Magnette were certainly not. I couldn't shake off my fascination with pedigree models of the past, (not that I wanted to) and the 1956 Jaguar was my latest choice and the MG's replacement.

My Jag was well past its prime although mechanically still performing to a breathtaking standard. The combination of high performance, disintegrating body and generally questionable roadworthiness made it a real challenge to drive. It had radial tyres on the front and cross-ply on the back – I have since learnt this was the wrong way round if the mixing of tyre types was to be entertained at all and extremely dangerous. The passenger door was held shut by an ingenious use of a stout length of rope attached to the door at one end and tethered at the other to an anchorage point in the middle of the car. The door did close and wasn't a problem until the car encountered an unexpected hump or pothole in the road. When this occurred, the excessively heavy door was likely to bounce off its catch as a result of the sudden jolt and swing open. The anchorage point was good and solid in distinct contrast to most of the rest of the vehicle. The rust-to-metal ratio must have been close to evens, but its most dangerous and unnerving characteristic was due to a braking system still reliant on drums on all four wheels, rather than discs. Fierce braking at speed caused the brakes to fade so badly sometimes, that the brake pedal ended up lifeless on the floor. The only remedy to this disconcerting predicament was to furiously pump the pedal until life returned to the system like a cardiac arrest patient receiving CPR.

It was without doubt a hair-raising car to drive and the exhilarating journeys to our concert venues all over the country live on in my memory as good ones. I'm happy to say that no untoward incident ever resulted from what in hindsight looks like a very reckless way to have behaved but in those days of no MOTs, empty roads and no speed limits on motorways, attitudes to road safety were vastly different from today. (In the Republic of Ireland, you could even drive unaccompanied without having taken a driving test as late as 1964.)

I went on to own two more Jaguars, a Mark 1 and a Mark 2 and just before leaving Belfast for good, I bought as an investment a dilapidated 1937 MG VA with a drophead coupe, Tickford conversion. I put it in the hands of a retired car worker appropriately named Austin, who had worked with this model as a young man on the MG production line and paid him good money in advance to do a complete restoration. To cut a long story short, he let me down badly, constantly asking for more cash, which I obligingly coughed up and for which he did little work in return. By the time I left Belfast, Austin had thrown in the towel and I was forced to leave the car, sitting unfinished, rotting in a barn on some remote farm complex. A year or so later, well after my departure, a surveyor visiting the farm uncovered the car, contacted me and made a derisory offer to buy it. I decided to cut my losses and reluctantly accepted, saying farewell to a frustrating and expensive episode.

One car-related memory from my time in Northern Ireland was decidedly not a happy one and one which had a profound influence on our approach to further escapades on the road. A local horn player, who was a regular extra with the orchestra, was tragically killed in a car crash when only in her twenties.

The Troubles were about to ignite, as more and more violent incidents took place amid the fomenting political instability and these incidents were of an increasingly threatening nature. In the early hours of March 1st, 1970 I was woken by the sound of a huge explosion coming from the other side of the city. A statue of the Reverend Hanna was no more, blown to smithereens by the Irish Republican Army. This seemed to cross a line in the level of violence being perpetrated. The main reason I wanted to move on was the level of dissatisfaction I was experiencing in the orchestra with Northern Ireland's political instability a contributory factor.

Like every orchestra, we had many guest conductors and soloists who provided variety and innovative ideas to savour, but it's the principal conductor who has to be relied upon to engender a lasting, productive and happy atmosphere. Communication, integrity, musicality and style are some of the necessary prerequisites in order to keep morale ticking over nicely.

Maurice Miles, the original principal conductor and founder of the orchestra, quickly moved on when it became apparent to everyone, including himself to his credit, that a younger more dynamic and visionary conductor was now needed to harness the orchestra's full potential. We found what we were looking for in the Romanian conductor, Sergiu Comissiona. In his late thirties, Sergiu was just starting out on what would turn out to be an illustrious international career having already been principal conductor of Romanian National Opera and the Haifa Symphony Orchestra, he later became principal conductor of both the Baltimore and

Gothenburg symphony orchestras, the Netherlands Radio Philharmonic and the RTVE Symphony Orchestra in Madrid. With Sergiu we went through a period of consolidation, giving many performances of a rewardingly high standard and began to discover our own distinct voice. The well-being of the orchestra was now in safe hands and morale at an all-time high, but a conductor of Sergiu's calibre will always be in great demand and after two years he departed. Following a period in limbo, his replacement was found, also Romanian but unfortunately, not from the same mould.

I took an instant dislike to Edgar Cosma in his ubiquitous cotton roll neck sweaters. (He must have visited the same image consultant as Neville Marriner.) I suspected Cosma felt the same way about me but at least I didn't wear my glasses over my ears rather than behind, an eccentricity his total baldness only helped to exaggerate. Perhaps he had a physical condition which required this weird positioning but because of his arrogant, unfriendly and distant demeanour, my sympathy was in short supply and I matched his arrogance by never satisfying any curiosity I might have had.

I loathed everything about the man, from his appearance to his mode of music-making. He reminded me of one of those toy cars, which when pulled backwards then released, sprints forward in a short burst of speed. No deviation of line, pre-programmed and utterly boring. Every result the same as the previous; each winding, producing a day's worth of dissatisfaction. Enough, time to go. I'm off to Norway. . .

EIGHT

A variation on the All-Day Breakfast, courtesy of a conscientious landlady – a handy suggestion for saving on expenses.

I always had a hankering to live abroad, with the Scandinavian countries high on my list. The appeal of absorbing another culture and discovering its unique identity was the driving force behind this urge. I had already glimpsed through modest trips abroad and frequent contact with foreign colleagues, that life abroad was quite different. The alternative of staying at home and taking the more normal path was not going to satisfy my spirit of adventure. So I set about making a move in that direction.

I had made a tentative effort a few years earlier, when myself and Duncan, a colleague and fellow violinist, approached Sergiu Comissiona and enquired about the possibility of joining one of three other orchestras of which he was also principal conductor. He was extremely encouraging and generously offered us places in all three. It was a case of *Take your pick*. The orchestras in question were the

Baltimore, Gothenburg and Haifa Symphony orchestras, three extremely attractive and tempting offers.

At that time, I was still very content with life in Belfast and decided after a good deal of thought, to postpone a move, leaving Duncan to decide whether it would be North America, the Middle East, or Scandinavia. He plumped for a position in the Gothenburg orchestra.

Fifty years later, Duncan has recently retired from that orchestra after spending his entire career there, bar his year in Belfast and a year in Bristol before that. He still lives there with his boat, two children close by and his Russian wife, who he spent two years extracting from the USSR, having met her there in 1985 while on tour with the orchestra.

I greatly admired the Scandinavian political and social systems and was particularly drawn to Norway as a destination and the Harmonien Orchestra based in Bergen with a lineage dating back to 1765 making it one of the oldest orchestras in the world (it has since been renamed The Bergen Symphony Orchestra). There were many reasons for this. I thought Norway's version of socialism, adhering rigorously to democratic principles, worked very well. The Norwegians grumbled and groaned about their high taxation rates, but generally, there was a willingness to pay, as they seemed to understand the necessity of losing such a hefty percentage of their income in exchange for the creation of a largely, equal society. This meant they also avoided most of the extremes of rampaging capitalism with all its dreadful inequality.

The standard of living was high and its people had a palpable communal spirit, producing perhaps, the most successful society in the world. I also loved the way the population revelled in its natural surroundings by embracing the outdoor life and I felt a kindred spirit with the Scandinavian psyche, gleaned from its distinctive literature, cinema and music. (Sibelius is my favourite symphonic composer.)

I found the Norwegians to be romantic and open-minded, but at the same time having a rather pessimistic view of the human predicament. They seemed resigned to their lot in some unfathomable way and consequently melancholic by nature. Their emotions ran deep and were hidden most of the time, but they would always welcome the chance to liberate their lighter side.

The city of Bergen comprises a double naturally shaped working harbour, sheltered in a complex of fjords and watched over by the friendly mountain of Floyen and the taller and more austere, Ulriken. I spent my first two weeks staying in a private house close to Bryggen, an area of mainly Hanseatic League trade buildings made of timber – a UNESCO heritage site – by the waterfront, where I had a rented room much like theatrical digs. I was the only guest and treated very well.

My breakfast was brought to my room every morning by the chain-smoking landlady and it was huge. It contained more than I could consume in one sitting, so rather than have what I couldn't consume returned to the kitchen, I removed it from the plates and secreted it in a drawer to supplement my evening meal which I was providing for myself. This continued over a few days with each subsequent day producing an even larger amount of food. It did strike me that my empty plates were giving a message to my landlady that not enough food was being provided. Nevertheless, my squirreling behaviour continued for a couple more days as I couldn't believe that breakfast could possibly further increase in size. But I was wrong, breakfast grew exponentially. I was now accumulating enough from each breakfast's leftovers to give me another complete meal. The moment had now come to own up and to my great relief, the landlady was perfectly understanding and the embarrassment was minimal. I reckon she was a mother, who in earlier days had brought up a family of her own and her maternal instinct had kicked in as she sympathetically recognised the plight of a young man, alone and new to a foreign land. The expansion element was now removed, but the generous breakfasts continued, slightly reduced but still of unfinishable portions.

The orchestra's week was short, one four-hour-long rehearsal per day, Monday to Thursday, with the only concert of the week at seven-o-clock on Thursday evenings. The concert could never be longer than one hour, forty-five minutes, as Bergen's only concert hall doubled as Bergen's only cinema and the films began at nine o'clock. With only fifteen minutes available for the transformation back to a cinema, there was no hanging about after these concerts. The miniscule workforce put into action a well-practised operation, removing and stashing all orchestra accoutrements effortlessly, lowering the screen and hey presto, a seamless transition from Mozart to Elvira Madigan.

We did have one or two other commitments throughout

the year; educational work and the occasional afternoon show for children. Otherwise we had the luxury of an eighteen-hour week and a three-day weekend. In the plentiful free time, I familiarised myself with Bergen and on the first of these days this was made more agreeable by doing so in the company of a journalist from New York who was taking a holiday touring Europe. We had struck up a conversation while sitting on a bench by the fish market down at the harbour and took it from there.

My standard of bridge is pretty rudimentary, but I'm keen and discovered to my delight that Bergen had a thriving Bridge Club. The club operated an open evening once a week, an evening when non-members were encouraged to participate and so, one evening I summoned up courage and went along. With my limited skills I was quite anxious in this unknown territory and made more so by a rumour floating about that Omar Sharif's Bridge partner was in attendance: the rumour turned out be true.

I got my nervousness under control and with my partner for the evening, another visitor, we circulated the room with all the other circulating pairs, moving from one table to the next and playing a hand against the stationary pair resident at each table. The evening passed happily, without me making a complete idiot of myself as far as I could make out and we didn't come up against the dreaded, celebrated visitor who must have also been part of one of the circulating pairs. I was wearing a highly patterned shirt, which by the end of the evening acquired further decoration in the form of a small hole in one of its cuffs as a memento of the evening. At some point in the proceedings, in a distracted state of anxiety, I had managed to hold my lit cigarette in such a way and for long enough, to burn a hole right through the cuff.

I was enjoying the orchestra. After four years in a chamber orchestra, it was refreshing to come face to face with the symphonic repertoire for the first time as a professional. I was also enjoying, after many years as a principal player, both as professional and student, relaxing at the back of the 2nd violins. I shared a desk with Philip, another English violinist of the same age and my flatmate: for what it's worth, we were both born in Norwich, as was Gerry, my desk partner in the Ulster Orchestra.

Norfolk: famous for Colman's mustard, dumplings, bishy barnabees and 2nd violins!

Any fears I might have had of being stranded abroad unable to understand the language were irrelevant. In the orchestra there were at least seven native English speakers and numerous other nationalities whose common language was English. English was also the common language as a means of communication for the many international guest conductors. As for the Norwegians, their English was phenomenal on the whole and spoken with little or no trace of accent, 'Yumbo Yet' being the most noticeable exception.

Rolf Dahl, the principal bass was the class act when it came to speaking English. In his thirties and never having lived outside Norway, he managed to put everybody else's English to shame, including the English. He sounded like an Old Etonian straight out of Oxford University, with faultless grammar and a vocabulary so comprehensive that the meaning of some words eluded me entirely. He was a fascinating character altogether. It was obvious that playing the bass was an unfulfilling profession for someone so extremely well read and of such high intelligence and the frustration resulting from such acuity fuelled his alcoholic tendencies which he was constantly in battle with. He was utterly stimulating company and a good friend to have made.

NINE

A well-balanced performance can be as influential as the work/life. balance. 'Bring on the timps!'

Christmas 1970 comes around and as much as I would have liked to experience a Norwegian Christmas, a two-week break from the orchestra gave me ample time to travel back to England to continue an unbroken run of Christmases with my parents.

I was in a delicate state of mind, torn between two women. Do I return to a relationship of four years standing with Niamh, or develop a newly formed relationship in Bergen which would take me in a completely different direction?

The summer I set off for Norway, Niamh and I had decided that time apart would be beneficial, further agreeing that by the Christmas, we either call it a day, or get back together. Our relationship had gone rather stale and a break seemed like a sensible course of action. That situation alone would make it difficult enough but now I had the added complication of having fallen in love with Anna, the principal conductor's daughter. Coming to a decision was not something I was looking forward to. And to top it all, Niamh and I were spending Christmas together with my parents.

I travelled back to England on the overnight ferry from Bergen to Newcastle, a twenty-four-hour journey, sharing a two-berth cabin with a stranger who little knew what was in store for him. He was about to witness the release of my pent-up emotions in startling fashion.

The cabin had no portholes as it was below the water line and no window to the corridor. With the light switched off, it was devoid of all natural light. I have never liked sleeping in a totally dark room at the best of times and in my emotionally fragile condition, this phobia was about to be unconsciously exaggerated.

Time for bed can no longer be put off and we take to our bunks for what would normally be termed, settling down for the night. I very often remember my dreams in great detail and tonight's dream of remarkable pertinence, will be no exception.

The Dream: I am heading for my cabin deep in the bowels of a boat, in the company of a roommate who is leading the way. We reach our cabin which is entered through two doors, the first of which my companion opens. He takes one step down into the tiny space between the doors, opening the second door in front of him. He then steps up and enters the cabin. I follow him by stepping down into the space between the two doors and simultaneously we close our respective doors behind us, leaving me suddenly in the pitch dark. Unable to open either door, I'm overwhelmed by feelings of claustrophobia: Edward Woodward in The Wicker Man would have understood, or more appositely, the owner of the head in Scream by Edward Munch. Now overcome by sheer panic, I begin pounding on the cabin door and yelling, 'Let me out, let me out.'

My dream comes to an abrupt end as I am now awoken by my unnerved cabin mate in almost the same state of fear as me. 'What the hell are you doing?' he yells. Well, what I am doing is precisely what I've been dreaming. I'm standing at our badly damaged cabin door, pummelling on it with the splintered remains of a wooden coat hanger clenched firmly between my fists and yelling.

I'm not prone to sleepwalking, but around that time, three or four other instances of a sleep-walking nature took place, which I'm sure a Freudian psychoanalyst wouldn't find too taxing to unravel.

For all my love of Norway and its people, I felt something crucial was missing from life there. I was not sure what and this was niggling me. Could it be that the society was just too well ordered, too hygienic? Scrubbed so clean, it's been sanitized into neutrality. I longed to hear a national deluge of barking dogs disturbing the peace, or someone venting their anger in public. A dirty street would be welcome, or a pair of shoes left in the middle of a living room floor, even a lost watch, found and not handed in. Anything to break the docile order of things.

As the ferry entered the mouth of the Tyne, I went up on deck, fully recovered from my nocturnal exertions and after five months of living in the paragon world I had just left, revelled in the sight of the imperfect scene slowly unfolding before me along the banks of the river and instantly realised that yes, this is what I had been missing. Dilapidated buildings, collapsing wharves and perished car tyres, plastic containers and supermarket trolleys poking out of the muddy, unkempt riverbank at crazy angles like bean shoots pushing their heads through the topsoil. Evidence of the existence of earlier life: rotting away it might have been, but a reminder everywhere I looked, of the continuum of life. Society ticking the *I am not a robot* box.

The truth is that perfection can be boring, even in music. Amongst us professional musicians, it's not uncommon to hear voiced a preference for a performance by an individual that betrays the fact it's a human being who is playing. Questionable personal taste and even the slightest of technical errors can help relate the listener to the performer in a much more human way. A risky tempo that doesn't quite work, an over accented passage or contentious choice of phrasing can all remind a listener in the midst of a sublime piece of music of the fallibility of the performer, a person much the same as yourself, who could well be sitting next to you in the pub before the evening's out.

The unexpected can be thrilling too. By taking liberties with the music score, the conductor at a concert in Timisoara of the Banatul Philharmonic Orchestra I recently attended, successfully transformed Schumann's 4th symphony into a timpani concerto. The magnificent timpanist towered over proceedings. Raised one level above the orchestra, he was mounted centre stage at the back on a rostrum and surrounded by his timpani which resembled devotees worshiping at the feet of their guru, but what really turned it in to a concerto was his body language and the balance between him and the rest of the orchestra. His dynamic range throughout, was at least thirty percent louder than normal and his choreographed antics emphasised his understanding of his role as soloist. This was really unusual and impossible to classify as a perfect performance of Schumann's 4th symphony as it didn't adhere to the normally accepted instrumental balance associated with the piece and presumably stipulated by Schumann in the score. The performance was impeccable in every other way and I smiled all the way through this irreverent interpretation.

By the time Christmas with my parents was over, Niamh and I decide to get back together and remained so for a further twenty-nine turbulent years.

Each Easter, the population of Bergen heads for the mountains and fjords, leaving it almost deserted apart from a few tourists. On Niamh's arrival a few days short of Easter 1971, I had planned to profit from the city's tranquil state by introducing her to the delights of the empty city. Central Bergen is compact and easily explored on foot, so conditions were ideal.

But just as Easter week arrived, news came that Niamh's father was seriously ill in hospital and unlikely to live more than a few days, so she immediately returned to Dublin. Suddenly, finding myself alone in an abandoned city, I decided to be positive and try to turn the unforeseen circumstances to my advantage.

Bergen's two main harbours are a constant hive of activity, from fishing boats to international ferries and everything in between. It's an important hub and staging post for the communities which rely heavily on sea transport along Norway's vast meandering coast. The many towns and small seaports thrive with the help of a large variety of cargo boats. These vessels ply their trade round the clock supplying the necessary goods as they pick their way in and out along the indented coastline like homeless pieces of a jigsaw puzzle searching by trial and error to find the right place.

As Bergen is central to this activity, it struck me that its harbour complex might be a fruitful source of an adventure. A trip northward on some type of sailing vessel would be the very thing. I was aware that it was possible to get a berth on some cargo boats at a fraction of the cost of a conventional ferry and with this in mind, I wandered down to the waterfront to try my luck. Nothing came of my first couple of enquiries apart from directions to a particular boat that I'm told might well fit the bill. I approached it with optimism and to my amazement, the captain, who of course spoke English, said he had a spare cabin which I could have if I was prepared to work my passage. This sounded more of an adventure than I had anticipated so I instantly agreed.

Before setting sail that evening, I hastily packed a bag, even remembering easily forgotten essential items like toothbrush, camera and pyjamas. I did overlook one thing though, a bottle of something alcoholic to sip when the appropriate moments arose. The captain had none on board, but he did suggest a contact on the quayside who might be able to oblige. So, on my behalf and with my consent he organised the purchase of a reassigned empty Coca-Cola bottle filled with aquavit. Through the porthole of my cabin, I observed the shady transaction, which was sealed by an extortionate amount of money passing hands and the dodgy vendor taking an enormous swig from the bottle before handing it over. I complained about the seller's greed to the captain once the bottle was safely in my hands, who calmly suggested by implication that to try and improve the deal would be more than my life was worth, or something along those lines. I had at least got what I wanted, even though it had cost an arm and a leg and possibly a nasty dose of a contagious virus.

The boat was a fair size at about seventy metres long and carried an eclectic mix of goods. Building materials such as timber, heavy machinery, light machinery, household goods and a tractor tethered to the deck.

There was no work for me on the first day, but as the boat sailed north, members of the crew were dropped off at their various hometowns for Easter, leaving the boat short-handed and temporarily in the hands of a novice crew member. My employment was restricted to one duty, that of steering. This sounded like a daunting task, but to my great relief, turned out to be quite straightforward. The boat's method of guidance was via a short and insignificant looking metal joystick, which when clicked once left or right, sent an electronic signal to the rudder, which turned the boat a miniscule amount in the desired direction. The delay between my action on the bridge and the subsequent realignment of the vessel was a little disconcerting at first and needed getting used to, but came soon enough. My instructions from the captain were simple. Keep the boat on a given sightline – a lighthouse, a church steeple, a buoy, or some such until he designated a new landmark. He checked on me about every ten minutes or so, otherwise I was left unattended. During these short periods of isolation I was often beset by moments of irrational fear, imagining a large oil tanker suddenly looming up out of nowhere and overcome by sheer panic, going on a clicking spree and losing control of the vessel.

The work schedule was a novel experience for me. I was obliged to work a shift of six hours followed by six hours of sleep, thus telescoping the pattern of a normal twenty-four-hour-day into twelve hours (I thought the worldwide trend was to shorten the working week rather than extend it to fourteen days). The boat operated continuously, either sailing or loading and unloading when docked. My schedule was maintained whichever circumstance prevailed and my six-hour-long work shift sometimes occurred when in port. I was then able to explore whatever little fjord town we were docked in, albeit on occasion, at rather strange hours. Being so far north at that time of year guaranteed nights that were short and remained relatively light. Roaming the deserted streets of a picturesque seaport at an ungodly hour, as the sun rose over the fjord and the snow-capped mountains was a magical experience.

The arrangement I had with the captain, was that in exchange for my steering duties, payment would be made in kind by providing me with food and lodging. As adventure was my goal and not as my father would say, 'the pursuit of filthy lucre', I was happy with the deal.

Only two cabins are allocated for passengers and the other one is already occupied by someone who had embarked in Stavanger, the starting point of the vessel's journey. I am told by the captain that my fellow passenger is heading for Trondheim for Easter and he's a paying customer. Two characteristics soon become obvious pertaining to my fellow traveller. Firstly, he suffers from vociferous nightmares of which I'm made fully aware, as our cabins are only separated by a thin bulkhead. He shouts his way through the night, peppering his disturbed outbursts in Norwegian with a constant cry of STOP! STOP! in English. Secondly, he is a hermit. Plates of food are systematically left at his cabin door, with the empty plate then reappearing sometime later in pristine condition. (Maybe he's an ex-convict with a lingering habit?) I don't see him the first couple of days, but at lunchtime on the third day our paths cross. As I arrive at my cabin door, his door opens and still dressed in pyjamas and dressing gown, he deposits his empty plate on the floor in the passageway. He doesn't shy away as I expect and the only two passengers on the boat strike up a conversation. In English, naturally.

It's another one of those extraordinary moments in my life, when more than mere coincidence seems to be at play. He is a seventy-year-old teacher who has returned to teaching after retirement and is now working in a supply capacity due to national shortages. This doesn't appear to be the most perspicacious decision he has ever made, considering the state of his troubled mind. His worries over his lack of control of his pupils are haunting his nights and manifesting themselves in these nocturnal emissions.

My fellow passenger turns out to be a music teacher and unlikely as it seems, his principal instrument is the violin. Our conversation soon reveals that in his cabin he has a double case containing two violins. Before long we are tuning the instruments and squeezed between the door to his cabin and bunk bed, we attempt to play as much of Bach's double violin concerto as we can remember. A perfect example of ships that pass in the night, complete with nautical context.

I don't see him again, but each night until his embarkation in Trondheim, the battle with his unruly and non-compliant class continues unabated as he barks out orders in his sleep.

Our trip back to Bergen was fast, as the captain was eager to return to his home base of Stavanger for what remained of the Easter break. We made a couple of brief stops, off-loading the few remaining units of cargo picked up during the northerly direction of the journey.

As this adventure neared its end and we glided over the becalmed water, a final image among many from the trip of the surrounding majestic mountains reflected upside down in the fjord's sheen made such an astounding visual impact that it remains with me to this day.

TEN

Colleagues can enhance your professional life in surprising ways – not to mention thrilling and sometimes hazardous.

Exuding such warmth and affability, it was surprising to discover that Norwegians were not great at creating humour themselves, but if an outside source was to encroach on their melancholia, they would welcome the intrusion with open arms.

The weekly Thursday concerts in Bergen were predictably earnest affairs. The audience's unerring regard for tradition and protocol made it feel like a form of religious devotion and so it was unlikely in the orchestra's 250-year existence, that from within the orchestra an organised but unscheduled humorous distraction had ever taken place during a performance. Phillip and I decided that the time had come to rectify this omission after noticing that Elgar's 'Pomp and Circumstance March No.1' was on the season's programme. The piece was an ideal vehicle for a chance to stimulate the Norwegians' funny bones.

Anyone familiar with the Henry Wood Promenade concerts which take place yearly in London's Royal Albert Hall will know that the final concert of the two-and-a-half-month-long series always culminates in a rendition of this Elgar march, including audience participation. The music is set to words of a song written in 1902 by A.C.Benson, 'Land of Hope and Glory' which extols, in the most jingoistic terms, the might of the old British Empire. The words plus the music combine to create a more emotive alternative British National Anthem and is quite possibly the most emotionally charged piece of British music – for the British – ever written. ('Nimrod' from Elgar's Enigma Variations and 'Dido's Lament' by Purcell are more worthwhile emotional journeys provided by British composers.)

Phillip and I have selected our moment of diversion to take place during the roof-raising final stanza and have prepared a tongue-in-cheek tribute to the Last Night, in what we hope will be an obvious, self-deprecating delivery. We have bought a couple of carnations for our buttonholes which we conceal under handkerchiefs draped over our left shoulders (not a suspicious look, as it's not unusual for violinists to protect their jackets in this way from wear and tear from the violin rubbing against the jacket's material). We also borrow a tea towel in the design of a Union Jack from Michael Titt, 2nd flute, another Englishman.

The concert proceeds and at the appropriate moment mid-performance we take to our feet, place our violins on our now vacated chairs and remove the handkerchiefs. We now stretch the tea towel between us with one hand and with the remaining free hand salute in the most pompous manner we can muster.

We have a certain amount of apprehension about how our actions will be received by both orchestra and audience, but it soon becomes clear this is unfounded. A gentle ripple of approbation runs through the audience, but more rewarding is the sight of a paroxysm of barely suppressed laughter within the orchestra, including our principal conductor, Karsten Andersen, who with diplomatically subtle body language, lets the audience know what has just occurred is more than acceptable.

Having endeared ourselves to the orchestra in no small measure, our popularity soared and the resultant celebrity became a passport to even greater acceptance and further invitations to social activities, some more surprising than others. One such invitation came from Hans, the 3rd flute/piccolo player who was an amateur pilot and through his obvious connection to Michael Titt, offered to take the British contingent of Michael, Phillip and myself on a sightseeing flight over Bergen and the surrounding fjords.

On the weekend chosen, the weather could not have been worse for flying, as minutes after the plane left the ground the conditions caused the airport to temporarily close. It's wet of course – Bergen has the highest rainfall in Europe – and the rain was accompanied by exceedingly high winds. As frightening experiences go, the take-off in this four-seater light aircraft was one of the worst of my life. Unsettling excessive noise and vibration were easily accommodated, but as the plane gained speed on the runway the sound escalated to an alarming clatter as the buffeting wind and driving rain made their presence strongly felt.

Fighting vigorously against the gusting wind, the plane's acceleration during its crab-like trajectory did eventually succeed in getting us airborne and in the few moments after finally detaching itself from the ground, the plane succumbed to a pattern of rising and falling in a state of confusion, not knowing whether to continue the battle or just give in to the overwhelming force of nature.

Somehow we did manage to stay in the air but the plane's antics were by then so out of kilter with any idea I had of flying that the encounter moved into the realms of the surreal and my fear transmogrified into resigned acceptance. A fly buzzing dementedly around a light bulb would have produced a more discernible flight path than ours. Hans remained calm throughout.

As we gained height, we also gained a degree of stability and I was beginning to enjoy myself. Glimpses of the obscured landscape below came and went through layers of cloud, but as the cloud thinned, vision improved enough for us to appreciate the uniqueness of what we saw beneath us. Hans said that flying in challenging conditions over Bergen was nothing new for him and added, 'What is unusual, is what I've just noticed in the fjord.'

He thought he had spotted a submarine on the water's surface but needed a closer look to be sure. We descended low enough for confirmation and happy with this rare sighting, together with the much-improved weather, he decided it was time to head back to Bergen's recently reopened airport.

The wind had dropped measurably but was still blowing enough to make our final approach an unnerving experience as the plane mimicked an autumn leaf's lightly swaying descent, uncertain when it will touch firm ground. But like the leaf, we landed gently and in one piece. The relief at being safely back on the ground was palpable and accompanied by profound exhilaration, the feeling that what you have just done is worthy of celebration. So, before our leave-taking over a beer or two, we reflected on our memorable flight, congratulated Hans on his expertise and for having provided excitement that had far surpassed all our expectations. For me, the modest celebration was more about relief at having survived, rather than any pleasure gained.

On the Monday morning, when the orchestra gathered for its ten-o-clock rehearsal, the atmosphere was distinctly different from usual. Gloomy and heavy laden. Members were clustered in small groups and muttering quietly amongst themselves with no sense of urgency to get the rehearsal underway. I was approached and asked, 'Have you heard about Nils?' Nils was a member of the 2nd violin section but nowhere to be seen this morning. 'He was out fishing with a friend in that awful storm on Saturday and he and his companion both drowned when their boat capsized.'

It transpired that the submarine we had seen was responsible for locating and recovering their bodies and without realising it, we had witnessed the final stage of the tragedy as it unfolded. Nils was a well-liked member of the orchestra of thirty years standing and his absence would be felt by all. A dramatic coda to our adventure and one that completely changed the complexion of that day's memory.

I had never skied so when the opportunity arose, I jumped at the chance. Ehrling, the 2nd oboe, had invited Michael, myself and Phillip, plus Norman the 2nd horn, to accompany him on a skiing trip to his holiday *hytte* in the hills. (The hut was grander than it sounds as it comfortably slept the five of us.) As a train journey was a necessary prelude to our exploit we arranged to meet at Bergen central station late one Friday morning on one of the orchestra's long weekends. Ehrling had talked enthusiastically about the impending trip for weeks and of his love of the outdoor life and it was obvious as we congregated at the station that his enthusiasm had kicked-in early. His weekend of leisure had started a good few hours in advance of our departure with a fair number of celebratory drinks already under his belt. Slurring his words and being unsteady of foot was a bit of a giveaway.

We boarded the train under a false impression that we were simply in search of suitable empty seats. Norman was leading the party, but Norman was not looking for any old empty seats. Earlier he had seen Miss Norway boarding the train and we were unknowingly in tow in his search for her whereabouts, in the hope that once found she would be surrounded by a sea of empty seats.

Norman was an American alpha male, built like a field athlete at six-feet-something tall, with dark, wavy hair and a brash, in-your-face manner. He was also under the delusion that he was irresistible to women, so he wasn't going to let a chance to impress a beauty queen pass easily.

Bingo! Norman located her and well up on his knowledge of beauty queens, confirmed that she was indeed Miss Norway.

Unperturbed by our invasion as we dutifully followed Norman into the otherwise empty compartment and settled down around her, the time was ripe for Norman to release his machismo and put his seduction technique to the test.

Ninety minutes later, we arrived at our destination with little change in the social status of those in the compartment. Ehrling is a tad more inebriated from having gently swigged throughout the journey from a bottle which he had secreted in a holdall slung around his neck (aquavit I would guess) and Norman's animal magnetism had failed to work the expected charms on the still poised and tolerant Miss Norway – she must have been mightily relieved to see the back of us.

The most hazardous leg of the journey was about to be undertaken. We had to negotiate on skis and laden with rucksacks, one kilometre in the dark. Fortunately, Michael and Norman took responsibility for most of the luggage, leaving the remaining trio of two complete novices and one experienced but alcoholically challenged sixty-year-old to fend for themselves.

We donned skis and set off. Phillip and I did surprisingly well with few spills, unlike the legless Ehrling, who performed a faultless impression of a toddler learning to walk, frequently toppling over and being assisted back upright. Norman and Michael acted as putative parents with stoical resignation, uprighting a tottering Ehrling every hundred metres or so. We eventually arrived at the hut, having covered the ground at what might have been considered a respectable time for a one-legged centipede.

For two days the sun shone constantly on the gleaming

pristine snow at this idyllic location, so I was able to get in plenty of practice and became quite proficient at cross-country, as opposed to downhill skiing. The evenings were equally enjoyable, with each day ending by sitting around a comforting log burning stove, which not only provided heat, but also a suitable ambience for lively banter and great conviviality. Platefuls of hearty food were rustled up by Michael and Norman, accompanied by the liberal consumption of beer and aquavit.

Ehrling's love of the outdoors however, had been in little evidence throughout the weekend, apart from two visits to the log pile. His drinking spree had continued unabated until shortly before our departure. (Fru Fjelli would be waiting at Bergen station and Ehrling will have to, at the very least, try to give the impression of being sober when meeting his wife.) Coinciding with his halt to drinking was the removal of his pyjamas which had been worn night and day since we arrived.

We departed on the Sunday afternoon by skiing from the hut back to the local station which turned out to a far more sedate exercise than that of two days earlier. Ehrling doggedly remained upright all the way, which was the only demonstration that he was capable of skiing at all.

Towards the end of my year in Bergen I read an advert for a vacancy in the only British orchestra I was interested in joining, a chamber orchestra called the Northern Sinfonia, based in Newcastle. Although I was all set to have a further year in Bergen, fate had intervened, causing me to reconsider.

The advert appeared just two weeks before the Northern Sinfonia's principal conductor, Rudolph Schwarz, was scheduled to conduct a Harmonien concert, so I felt compelled to apply for an audition. My application prompted an immediate response, suggesting that as Rudolph would be in Bergen in the next few days, the normal auditioning procedure of playing to a panel of principal players and conductor could be circumvented and I need only play to Rudolph there in Bergen and on his arrival I duly auditioned.

Auditioning simply involved playing a prepared solo piece of my own choice, followed by sight-reading three or four excerpts from the standard orchestral repertoire (these days, the orchestral excerpts are stipulated in advance and therefore prepared). The whole process was relaxed, finishing off with a casual chat.

The next day, Rudolph having reported back to the Northern Sinfonia, I received a telegram offering me a job, which I accepted.

Harmonien's generosity had been unbounded during the year. The orchestra had provided me with subsidised accommodation, paid for my violin strings and Union fees and fortuitously, was inadvertently covering the expense of repatriation back to the UK, as my final commitment to the orchestra was a ten-day tour of Britain.

I'm afraid the enduring memory of this final tour could provide yet another chapter on the theme of Musicians and their Overworked Bladders, but I will resist the temptation. Suffice it to say that so much beer was consumed during the tour's long coach journeys, exacerbated by celebrations for

Ergil, a double bass player for whom this tour would mark his retirement after a lifetime as a member of Harmonien, that the drivers became intolerant of the ever-increasing requests for lavatory stops. The stops were seriously interfering with the timetable and got to the point when they blankly refused to stop anymore. Let's draw a veil over the inevitable result involving empty bottles.

In my solitary year as a member of Harmonien, the friendliness and generosity of the Norwegians was best exemplified by having been invited to the homes of at least a third of my colleagues for some form of get-together. I was leaving the orchestra with a certain amount of regret, but with many happy memories which had made deep impressions, teaching me much along the way.

Newcastle upon Tyne now beckons.

ELEVEN

The joyful effect of music is so powerful that producing it as a way of passing time is hard to beat – especially as a 'happy amateur'.

I began my tenure with the Northern Sinfonia as principal 2nd violin but after three months my unhappiness in that position was met by an equal measure of dissatisfaction from my employers, making my association with the orchestra extremely precarious, if not terminal. Fortunately for me, the situation was salvaged when a timely vacancy arose in the 1st violins, which was then offered to me.

This reprieve amounted to much more than just good news at finding myself still in employment. The advert I had responded to when originally applying for a job in the Sinfonia wasn't for the position of principal 2nd, but for a rank-and-file 1st violin position. I really didn't want to return to the 2nd violins.

Being a member of the 2nd violins is all very well but is a little like the function of the left hand when playing at an elementary level on the piano, with 1st violins taking on the role of the right hand. 1st violins get the juiciest cuts of meat, leaving the 2nd violins with the bones and gristle, with an occasional bit of lean attached. 1st violins have the joy of playing glorious melodies.

I had enjoyed the relative relaxation of a year of sitting at the back of the 2nd violins in Bergen, but now was time for a change to membership of a 1st violin section and the excitement at the prospect of the musical and technical challenges that lie ahead.

How I became principal 2nd as a result of auditioning for a rank-and-file job turned out to be a little convoluted and was all to do with the orchestra involving itself in an exercise to save face. The position of principal 2nd had been vacant and constantly advertised for two years and the orchestra's management now felt it reflected badly on the orchestra's image that they had been unable to fill the position. They switched to advertising a 1st violin job instead, a position that didn't exist, in the hope of attracting someone suitable enough to fill the vacant principal 2nd job. So, after my audition as a 1st violin, it came as a complete surprise to be offered an entirely different position from the one I had applied for.

Hearing this explanation didn't alter my feelings about wanting to have a 1st violin job and I initially turned the job down. It was then suggested to me by the management that I should try out the 2nd violin position and if after three months I still wanted to play 1st violin, then I could do so (it was never explained how that would have been accomplished without a vacancy arising) and on that basis, I joined the orchestra.

Three months later, it all worked out to everyone's satisfaction, a vacancy in 1st violins did arise and I relinquished the post I never wanted in the first place and was more than happy to accept one I did want.

I inherited a seat vacated by Ronnie Birks, who was leaving for Sheffield, to join the Lindsay Quartet as 2nd violin, a position he remained in for forty years. During his time in Newcastle, Ronnie also led a quartet made up of Colin Callow and Robin Benefield, both members of the orchestra's 2nd violin section, with Robin swapping to the viola when playing in the quartet. The cellist was Michael Borthwick, a medical student nearing the completion of his studies and an exceptionally fine cellist, even by professional standards. Much to my joy, these three asked if I would like to take Ronnie's place in the quartet, which I did without hesitation.

The Linden Quartet as we called ourselves gave regular but infrequent concerts which were performed on the basis that we played for no financial reward, making ourselves available to anyone who was prepared to provide a platform and produce an audience. In essence, we played for nothing and if any profit was made from our performances from the sale of tickets, then the proceeds had to go to a charitable organisation or a worthy cause we approved of. We were also happy to perform as part of a celebration on condition the same monetary strictures were applied.

This all sounds wonderfully altruistic but altruism was secondary to our desire to explore performance environments divested of the usual concert pressures. We wanted to find out if removing a fee for playing would also remove most of the anxiety normally associated with performing, (at least for three of us) and thereby produce better playing. Four friends making music together in an intimate and relaxed setting, comfortable in the knowledge it was just for themselves and not in response to any reward other than personal satisfaction – a hark back to my Essex Youth Orchestra days.

Stage fright has dogged me my whole life, rarely feeling completely comfortable on stage. I would always have to make efforts to control my breathing before and after taking the stage and discipline myself whilst playing to check that I wasn't tensing muscles in my legs and shoulders, as well as making sure violin and bow were held using no more than the lightest grip necessary. A normal amount of performance nerves is no bad thing so long as it doesn't progress to a secondary stage of worrying whether the nervousness will get worse and develop into uncontrollable shaking. Bows have been known to clatter to the floor, travel to the wrong side of the bridge and even get trapped under the strings during a violently executed up bow. Left hands aren't immune to the onset of platform nerves either with fingers under a deluge of tension-produced perspiration behaving like an ice skater fighting to stay upright. The fingers of the left hand are also vulnerable to seizing up, as tension is the arch enemy, with stopping altogether as the darkest fear lurking somewhere in a performer's psyche.

Here's a bit of home-grown philosophy. When it comes to long lasting enjoyment and undiminishing gratification, making music is best done as a hobby. If stage fright could be removed along with other negative aspects that come automatically with being a professional musician, such as the setting of unrealistically high standards, time pressures, routine, etc., then you have a Happy Amateur.

Over the years, I've observed any number of amateur players, from very good to unbelievably bad, display perpetual exuberance at making music throughout their lives, even into their nineties. Of course, we pros are extremely lucky to be doing what originated as a hobby. We all start out, every one of us, for the love of playing, essentially as amateurs, with no thoughts about status or remuneration. Then, as time passes, an inevitable degree of cynicism creeps in and the divergence begins between professional and amateur.

There is possibly a simpler answer to the amateur's unceasing enthusiasm. Music is well known for its healing and restorative effect and is commonly used in therapy for people with mental health needs, dementia and Alzheimer's disease. Patients suffering from brain injuries, pregnant women during childbirth and the managing of chronic pain also benefit from the power of music.

Care homes and old people's homes get regular visits from visiting musicians, with music often being the only trigger able to unlock memories or free up emotions that normally lie dormant.

The joyful effect of music is so powerful that producing it as a way of passing time is hard to beat. And here's the nub of the hypotheses: the pleasure gained from making music is further enhanced for amateur players, as their hobby works as a perfect foil to whatever they might be engaged in professionally.

Perhaps the healing power of music is one reason so many amateur players I've met over the years have been practising medics – and they seem to have much in common with professional musicians.

Michael Borthwick, our Linden Quartet cellist, isn't the only doctor I count among my friends and not necessarily through being amateur musicians either. I reckon the reason for this is that musicians and medics are mutually compatible as they have so much in common professionally. Both professions necessitate a high degree of technical expertise and both use vocabularies particular to their professions (music having a whole, written language of its own). Both often work antisocial hours and require extended periods of concentration, with elevated levels of stress inherent to both. The stress also tends to be dealt with in the same way: humour and drinking to excess.

As patrons of the arts, medics are always well represented and a disproportionate number are amateur musicians. Many of whom attain remarkably high standards and are quite capable of undertaking performances at a professional level, anything from participating in orchestras to solo recitals. There are even orchestras made up entirely of doctors. The number of doctors who play instruments that I know personally, is staggeringly high.

Ian Kerr happens to be one of my closest friends and one such doctor. Our friendship dates back to 1975. As a polymath, perhaps it is not so surprising that he plays the piano. More impressive still, is that he excels as a pianist, gaining a London College of Music Performance Diploma (LLCM) in his sixties. This is equivalent to a final year of a music degree at a music conservatory. But don't get the impression that this practising medical psychotherapist's exam success is simply about achievement. Every day, only missing the odd day when a piano is not accessible, he mounts his piano stool and makes love to his beloved piano. I think another area which unites the two professions, is the strong influence their professions have on their emotions, although via totally different routes. And perhaps the two areas where they mostly diverge, is that of remuneration and intellectual ability (with a few exceptions, in both professions). However, any disparity between the two is easily overcome and consolidated by a healthy amount of mutual fascination.

A final word on the importance of the Linden Quartet: it did more than just work as a rewarding leisure pursuit; as we shall soon see, one of our performances four years later became the catalyst for the most significant episode of my professional life.

During the Sinfonia's 1974-75 season, it undertook a lengthy six-week tour of South America and the Caribbean. The tour was unremarkable from any musical perspective, more a holiday of discovery disguised as hard work. Nine different countries, two concerts a week and only two popular programmes featuring a soloist in each. At the end and beginning of the tour the solo work performed was *Les nuit d'ete*, a song cycle by Hector Berlioz with Sandra Browne as soloist and Manoug Parikian played Mozart's violin concerto in A major during the middle three weeks. The programmes needed minimal rehearsal time to keep them up to scratch (usually short seating rehearsals of no more than half-an-hour). This generated a luxurious amount of leisure time.

Everything is organised in advance on such a tour: travel arrangements, accommodation and most of your food. You just had to be at the right place at the right time to either play or be transported, allowing the assembly to progress unimpeded.

The tour was primarily financed by and under the auspices of the British Council and we were extremely fortunate to have had the opportunity to undertake such a tour. Today, mainly due to the tightening of finances within the Arts and the necessity for a greater degree of accountability, such sybaritic tours are most unlikely to happen.

As we would be visiting no cold climates, lightness of travel was easily achieved, always a serious consideration when encumbered by a musical instrument. Another necessary consideration to be made was deciding on the size of my suitcase and what to take. I tried to anticipate the demands on its capacity as the tour progressed and allow space to accommodate the inevitable swelling collection of ineluctable mementoes.

Apart from the official concert attire, I opted for a couple of traditional shirts, a few T-shirts, an embarrassingly small number of underpants which could look forward to frequent washdays and two pairs of dungarees: these could be adapted when something more formal was called for, by discarding the detachable braces and stuffing the then flapping bib down the front of the trousers behind the flies. Perfect.

Up until that time, my experience of other cultures had been limited to those similar to that of England; holidays in Europe, one year in Norway and four years in Northern Ireland. But this trip exposed me to a considerable number of diverse societies over a relatively brief period, an exposure I was never likely to encounter again. Each day brought its own revelations, the most striking being the disparity between rich and poor and the apparent ease with which the two lived closely side by side. It was the first time I had come face to face with real poverty in all its grim and shocking manifestation and it made a lasting impression.

Brasilia is a wonder architecturally. Futuristic buildings set well apart, dominate the landscape, connected by a mind-boggling road system. The wide streets give the impression of open space, helped by the comparatively low-rise buildings, which although imposing in scale, are not the usual, soulless, towering blocks of anonymity. The populace is dwarfed by this modernity and seems to have been relegated to an almost insignificant role making the relationship between buildings and people different from anywhere else I have seen.

Brasilia reminded me of a 1966 National Board of Canada short, animated film which imagines Martians observing our planet and coming to the conclusion that vehicles were the controlling force and people were machines carrying out their instructions. I think the extra-terrestrials were probably hovering above Brasilia at the time.

On one of our free days, the orchestra was invited to a garden party at the British Ambassador's residence. The building is suitably grand, with a large, empty expanse of lawn for a garden. Tables laden with a vast selection of finger food and beverages are laid out on the grass close to the house, with the rest of the lawn stretching out about fifty metres, to a metre-high boundary wall. Once the party is well under way, I make a break for freedom and wander down to the bottom of the garden. The other side of the wall is uncultivated as far as the eye can see, a sandy soil anchoring a few thirsty looking bushes and as I take in these desert-like features, my eye is caught by something strange up against the far side of the wall. On closer observation, I realise that I'm looking at a terrace of make-shift cardboard dwellings running the length of the wall and people are living there. I recoil in shock, feeling like a stranger who has accidentally intruded upon someone's private grief and abruptly retrace my steps and re-join the party, with its incongruously dressed, white-jacketed waiters. The contradiction is stark and the party suddenly seems completely out of place.

This experience will colour the rest of my tour as I now become constantly aware of privilege and deprivation juxtaposed everywhere we go, making me fully conscious in which camp I am firmly rooted and not just on this tour but back in Britain as well.

My reaction is not surprising, but neither is it particularly laudable. My epiphany of sorts doesn't lead me to renounce my present, privileged way of life and take to wearing sackcloth Gandhiesque style, but it does reinforce my already cynical attitude towards Authority, the Establishment, Officialdom or whatever else you might call it. I accept that Law and Order and some kind of institutionally based Democracy is what binds and holds a decent society together, but these very same institutions also control and perpetuate the status quo, acting as impenetrable structures of grandiloquence, doing little to advance conditions for the majority, as the divide between rich and poor ever widens. I'm reminded of a stunning rendition of a protest song I heard some years ago which moved me to tears. Since then I've listened to different versions of 'Which Side Are You On' written by Florence Reece in the 1930s, but none have had the same impact as that first one sung by Natalie Merchant.

A few days later we have another reception to attend, this time in Buenos Aires, given by the British Ambassador to Argentina. His speech welcoming us, our conductor and our two soloists is delivered in predictably diplomatic style, up to the point when mentioning the soloists. He glides effortlessly over Manoug Parikian's name which could possibly have caused a problem, then becomes hopelessly entangled over the final hurdle in his effort to remember the name of the other soloist. It's a memory lapse of sizeable proportions considering the circumstances: 'And finally, I would like to thank Sa... Sa... Sa... Ssan... Sand... er Ssandie... Sandie Shaw for honouring us.'

At this point, a loud cachinnation erupts, interrupting the ambassador's ramblings. This is followed by the orchestra bursting into a rendition of 'Puppet on a String'. The ambassador has inadvertently given away where his real cultural preferences lie and has blurted out the name of the singer of the United Kingdom's winning song in the Eurovision Song Contest some years earlier.

The spontaneous singing helps to lighten the mood, but the blunder is significant. Sandra Browne, the young, black and politically aware Trinidadian mezzo-soprano is understandably furious. She later confides in me she felt the incident encapsulated all the racial prejudice she had been struggling against all her life in the essentially *white world* of classical music and society at large. And, as a Trinidadian, I'm sure it's a painful reminder of the elitism of British colonialism. Sandra is the only surviving child of six and, ironically, after graduating was all set on a career in the diplomatic service but narrowly opted for life as a musician instead.

Sandra Browne had won the prestigious Kathleen Ferrier Memorial Competition in 1971 with a voice not that dissimilar to the great Kathleen Ferrier herself whose instantly recognisable singing distinguished her from other contraltos of world class. Even today, seventy years after her untimely death at the age of forty-one, that individuality still impresses.

Inimitability, whether instrumental or voice is what I savour most in a soloist, something perhaps more easily recognised amongst singers from the more popular genres of music, voices like those of Billy Holliday, Ray Davies and Amy Winehouse, whose voices appeal to me just as much as those of John McCormack, Cecilia Bartoli and Thomas Quasthoff.

The trumpet playing of Maurice Andre exemplifies what I mean when thinking of instrumentalists. Others who readily come to mind for their individuality of sound and musical perception include the violinist Fritz Kreisler, the flautist Jean Pierre Rampal and pianist Glen Gould.

We arrive in Chile at a time of political turmoil, in the aftermath of President Allende's removal by a *coup d'état* in 1973. The country is under the repressive control of General Pinochet's regime and on the brink of war with neighbouring Peru. We give two concerts, one in Santiago, a city with an all-pervading air of foreboding; the taste is bitter and generally unpalatable, which is exacerbated by having a night-time curfew in place.

The second concert is in the coastal city of Valparaiso, where I spend some of my plentiful free time strolling along an impressive beach. Substantial outcrops of spiky, sand-coloured rocks pepper the beach and large, loosely coiled waves pound the shore, offering a much-needed sense of liberation on this brief, but long-enough, visit to Chile.

Flying into Lima seated in the cockpit is a new experience for me. The age of aviation terrorism has yet to arrive and it wasn't unusual on request for a passenger to be allowed on the flight deck of a commercial flight, simply for the thrill. The approach, low over the Pacific Ocean and the rising cliffs of the Peruvian coast is especially spectacular from this advantageous position, even though it's tinged with trepidation; a sensation perhaps familiar to a guest conductor faced with a large, unfamiliar orchestra at a first rehearsal.

The bus journey from airport to city centre provides yet another spectacle of the air. Pelicans cruising at rooftop height above the busy road, provide an escort as they match the speed of the traffic below. The sight of these large, ungainly birds riding the air currents with such consummate ease is mesmerising, but to a Peruvian it must be no more extraordinary than drinking a decent cup of coffee.

For the duration of my stay in Lima, I am continually reminded of my surname. It's embellished in bold lettering on the side of a fleet of American style school buses which are ever-present during daytime hours: Markham College is an international independent school, founded by the British explorer and historian, Sir Clements Robert Markham. My family name is not so common and to see it displayed prominently so far from home, gives me an odd feeling of attachment and pride. It's frightening to realise how easily we can be manipulated.

On our way to Panama, we had a refuelling stop at Quito in Ecuador, a refuelling stop that almost became a hospital stop. The ancient propeller driven plane, in the thin air of one of the highest commercial airports in the world, got it slightly wrong and smacked into the runway at speed with such force it bursts two tyres. The plane, a degree out of control, was brought rapidly to a standstill by the application of heavy, emergency braking.

The rear of this superannuated aircraft had a seat configuration commensurate with its age and one more likely to have been found in the lounge bar of a pub back home. The rear row of seats ran the whole width of the cabin in a semi-circle and under these seats, some members of the orchestra had stowed their instruments. The vicious braking was alarming for all of us, but the sight of precious instruments shooting out from under some of these seats and hurtling at great velocity down the aisle was even more alarming. As good fortune would have it, no damage was done to either instrument or passenger. Ironically though, it was later found that a double bass, securely packed away in its protective case in the hold, had been damaged badly enough to warrant a visit to an instrument repairer.

The plane was hastily reshod and, nervously, we took to the air again.

I remember visiting the canal with its impressive lock system but remember little else of wonder about our visit to Panama City. What I do remember is not very flattering and possibly distorted over time. The conduit for this unflattering memory was probably the enormous American military presence, a presence that was due to the canal's strategic importance, both militarily and commercially. My impression was of a city suffering from the worst excesses of American culture; sleazy bars, seedy restaurants, strip clubs and tawdry shops lining run-down streets. Belligerent military personnel, obstreperous and often excessively drunk, thronged these thoroughfares, making it the least enlightening of all the places we visited on the tour.

Two years after a massively destructive earthquake hit Nicaragua in 1972, significant aftershocks from another earth-shattering event of a totally different nature are about to rumble through the capital, Managua.

Unlike most people, I have no memory of what I was doing when J F Kennedy was assassinated, but I certainly do remember what I was doing when Richard Nixon resigned. It's August 9th 1974 and having just given a concert in Managua, we are being feted by wealthy American and British members of the local community. It's being held in our honour, but the atmosphere is far from celebratory. The mood is being dictated by the predominantly American contingent, who are in a distracted state of agitation over the imminent denouement of the whole Watergate saga. They don't have to wait long; Nixon resigns before the night is out and the party winds down. Several Americans, mostly males, are now in tears, or close to tears. I can't help feeling that this reaction is excessive in its misplaced patriotism fuelled emotions that are insular and divorced from the larger global picture. Alongside religious intolerance, jingoism has to be responsible for most of the conflict that bedevils civilization. More evidence of the mind's willingness to be duped and manipulated.

The party breaks up and our hosts taxi us back to our hotel. The driver of the car I'm in is the burly American owner of the largest bookshop in Managua and possibly the owner of the largest and most vulgar car in Managua too. He's quite drunk and muttering tearfully about the night's event. He drives cautiously and suspiciously slow enough to attract attention. Luckily there are no police around to take heed of this, but his near somnambulism doesn't go unnoticed within the car.

The car has bench seats front and back; driver and two passengers in the front and four passengers in the back. A mischievous thought simultaneously crosses the mind of the two passengers seated next to the rear doors. Nick, the 2nd Bass and myself haul ourselves through the open windows on this barmy night and climb onto the roof unnoticed by the driver. I can't speak for Nick, but I'm sure my action is motivated less by the alcohol in my system than by my incredulity at the over-reaction of our hosts to the Nixon news.

In
Mexico,
1984

Lying flat on the car's roof, we edge far enough forward to be able to peer back into the car through the windscreen. Fortunately for us, the braking we prompt is a gentle, very sedated version of an emergency stop and we remain on the roof as the car comes to a halt. The driver is far too mentally troubled to think that anything out of the normal has just happened and simply waits for us to descend, board the car once more and continue our journey undramatically to the hotel. Our irresponsible antic pales into insignificance compared to the melodrama of American political fervour.

Mexico City comes and goes amid a background of happy street noise, colour, mariachi bands and a few insults directed at us by a random group of local males mistaking us for Americans.

TWELVE

Prone to falling asleep during rehearsals? 'Choose the double bass for comfort.'

We had just over a week before our return to Newcastle and, as the tour neared completion in the more laid-back Caribbean, the mood was noticeably lighter. And where an ambassador's reception was involved, decidedly more irreverent.

The British Ambassador in Jamaica throws a party in the garden of his colonial residence, a wooden building with appropriately curlicued ornamental terrace which stands Empire-proud as it oversees the lush vegetation of the garden below. For our delectation, the ambassador has assembled the great and the good of Jamaican society which includes politicians, academics and military personnel. By this point in the tour, my left-wing tendencies are tapped into quite automatically when faced with yet another reception and judging by those in attendance on this particular afternoon, automation is going to be immediate.

The backslapping soon gets underway and alcohol flows freely. Already half-cut, I somehow find myself chatting to the Minister for the Arts who brightly twinkles away at me. Mischievously I reciprocate and erroneously twinkle back in equal measure. Before I know it, he whips out his business card and an invitation to lunch the following day. I accept and he writes down the details of our assignation on the back of the card before we part company.

I move onto my next minister. She tells me she is the Minister for. . . I instantly forget which ministry, or more probably, don't take it in in the first place. We natter away innocuously until interrupted by the sound of the British National Anthem wafting from the terrace. Everyone falls silent, eyes turn towards the residence, where a highly decorated army officer stands, saluting throughout the anthem, where he blends into the colonial style surroundings in his colonial style uniform as though camouflaged for the occasion. It's really quite a comical scene, made all the more comical by this curious rendition of God Save The Queen. Its alternating pitch, which I presume is caused by an erratic turntable speed, is an unmistakeable characteristic of a wind-up gramophone.

The period piece comes to an end and I turn back to continue my conversation with the Minister of . . . and ask her, 'Who is that?'

'Oh, he's the Head of the Jamaican army,' she replies and I respond, 'He looks very young to hold such a position.'

'Well, he's a very good soldier,' is her explanation.

At this, like a dig in the ribs, a mental picture of my father looms up and I posit, 'Surely, there is no such thing as a *good* soldier.'

Her reaction is swift. Sensing a *red under the bed* and a conversation going in a direction completely unacceptable, she precipitately turns without uttering another word and quicker than I could down a Jamaican rum punch, the Minister of *Evasion* is gone.

I think I've suddenly turned into my father. Or, from beyond the grave, he's using me as his mouthpiece.

I need a drink. I grab a couple of gin and tonics from a passing tray, toss them back quickly and go in search of Nick, who once located, will I'm sure be in a similar frame of mind. He and I during the course of the tour have formed a bond of mutual understanding concerning receptions, although I suspect Nick's motives differ from mine in that his attitude is less cynical and probably more reflects the fact that he is just a hooligan.

Nick is easily found and with G&Ts in hand, we go exploring. We wander down the garden towards a shoulder-high hedge and discover to our absolute joy, a swimming pool on the other side. Without the need for affirmation, we immediately know where our obligation lies. The heat of the afternoon and my cynicism are at boiling point and we plunge fully clothed into the beckoning turquoise water as the lid lifts. From there, we raucously let off steam, having found the perfect antidote to *receptionitus*.

A few minutes pass before our raucous behaviour registers with the rest of the gathering and a sea of peering eyes appear above the hedge seeking out the source of jollification. Once curiosity is satisfied, the spying eyes withdraw leaving us to continue splashing about, exhilarated and impervious to whatever anyone might be thinking.

Chris Yates is a good egg. He manages the orchestra with calm efficiency and congenial manner and I should add, not the manager responsible for the fiasco surrounding my appointment to the orchestra. He is now standing beside the pool, endeavouring to entice us out of the water. After much encouragement, his persistence pays off and we climb out of the pool, briefly, before rebelliously launching ourselves straight back in. We eventually acquiesce after Chris invests a fair bit more perseverance and dedication to the task and we clamber out. By the time Nick and I make it to the coach which is taking the orchestra back to the hotel, the party is over and the rest of the orchestra is already on board. Sloshing our way, dripping wet down the aisle of the coach, we find ourselves the focus of the second reception of the day, a welcome one this time in the form of enthusiastic clapping with no allergic reaction.

Chris, true to character takes no disciplinary action, nor offers any harsh words and there are no negative repercussions at all.

Oh yes, my lunch date. On arriving back at the hotel, my conscience kicked in as I remembered what had been arranged for the next day, so I phoned the Arts Minister, apologised for my misleading behaviour in the garden and cancelled our lunch date. Extricating myself from the predicament was made slightly easier as luckily, I had only to deal with an answering machine.

Having just had a thrash around in a boisterous sea in the company of Chris and the Sinfonia's assistant manager, we found ourselves savouring a delicious plate of buttered lobster in a dilapidated café made of reeds. As we watched the lobster being readied in the barely anchored makeshift kitchen precariously balanced on an unstable pebble beach, I heard for the first time, 'Killing Me Softly' sung by Roberta Flack. She captures the mood of the song perfectly and the music fitted neatly into how I was feeling at the time and has moved me ever since. I think the lyricism is in the same league as that of 'The Windmills of Your Mind', another very effective song, but I can't help thinking that the slow movement of Mozart's Sinfonia Concertante had a hand in the latter.

The day of the final concert of the tour arrives and we are now in Port-of-Spain, Trinidad. The evening concert has a short rehearsal as usual, late in the afternoon and devoted mostly to a new arrangement by David Haslam (principal flute) of 'God Save the Queen'. Rather carelessly, three of us, David, Nick and I, had decided to meet at lunchtime that same day and sample a bottle of 50% proof Jamaican rum. Providentially, I fell asleep just before the appointed hour and missed the tasting, but the other two were not so fortunate. They had met as arranged and turned the tasting into full consumption, polishing off the whole bottle.

By the time of the rehearsal, they are both teetering on the edge of not being able to play. Both are in position however and prepared to give it a go.

Not long into the rehearsal, Nick falls asleep on duty, slumped over his double bass. He has to be prised from his instrument and sleep-walked from the stage, threaded through one of the many arches of the open-sided Queen Elizabeth Hall and laid down on the grass outside, all the while still fast asleep. The rehearsal goes on as though nothing has happened and David's arrangement of the National Anthem is about to get its first airing.

The wind section is raised on rostra with David at the highest and farthest point from the conductor, Norman del Mar. David seems to have fared better than Nick. He's awake and just able to play, but in cantankerous mood, persistently picking holes in Norman's interpretation of his precious arrangement. Norman must be well aware of the situation and takes it all in his stride as David constantly interrupts, bobbing up and down out of his seat to make each point. Every bob is a triumph of balance, until it isn't. . . One bob too many ends in a clatter and several gasps, as David, in mid-rant topples backwards off the rostrum taking his chair with him and disappears from sight. His pride is the only thing that is hurt and he bounces back, keen to continue from the point before the acrobatics took place. Norman, in his wisdom seizes the moment and appropriately deems the rehearsal over.

When we return for the concert, we walk past the recumbent and still slumbering Nick in the exact position on the grass he had been left in three hours earlier. He is occasionally checked to make sure he is still breathing, but otherwise remains in this position for the entire performance. Miraculously, David – presumably after drinking enough coffee to register a beneficial change to Trinidad's GDP that month – plays like a dream and even 'God Save the Queen' goes without a hitch.

Next morning, we head for home and not a moment too soon.

In the Spring of 1975, I was in Wylam, a village close to Newcastle where our Linden Quartet was giving one of its free performances. This one was not to raise money for a charity, but purely to celebrate a wedding anniversary taking place in the spacious home of the couple concerned. They were medical colleagues of Michael and the audience of fifty or so were close friends and family.

I was expecting this concert to meet with a better reaction than our first performance did three years earlier when Michael was still a medical student. He had arranged for us to play to a small number of his patients at St. Nicholas' psychiatric hospital in Gosforth where he was a Houseman at the time. We deliberately kept the programme short and only played Dvorak's popular quartet, 'The American'. At the end of the piece, instead of enthusiastic applause, there was a deafening silence which was broken after a few seconds by a woman on the front row loudly voicing her opinion in pure Geordie, 'Eh, that was aarful.'

The very cosy setting for this Wylam concert found us almost sitting on the audience's laps and beside a large open log-burning fire, which was spitting and crackling in the background as we performed. (The noise is clearly captured on a tape made of the concert.) We had brought along our friend Heather, a freelance viola player and wife of Ronnie Birks, the previous leader of the Linden Quartet. She was deputising with the orchestra for the week and was curious to hear how the quartet had fared in the last four years.

The evening went well and as we were leaving, Heather said to me, 'How would you like to join a full-time string quartet?'

I was intrigued by the question and thought it to be no more than an encouraging random enquiry. 'Have you ever thought, perhaps, of joining a professional quartet?' I answered lightly, 'Yes, I'd like that Heather, thanks very much.'

To my surprise she added, 'Well, the Edinburgh Quartet are looking for a 2nd violin right now. I know Michael Beeston very well, the viola player in the Quartet – Ronnie had been Michael's best man – and if you are interested in having a go, I'll ring him tomorrow morning, put him in the picture and tell him to expect a call from you later in the day. . .'

Within the week I was in Edinburgh, spending the day sight-reading through several pieces with what remained of the Edinburgh Quartet. At the end of the audition, having done myself reasonable justice, I expected to have to wait days, perhaps weeks to hear whether it had been enough to secure the position, but before hopping on a train back to Newcastle, Miles, the 1st violin thoughtfully asked if I would like to go for a meal, which I happily accepted.

Once in the Doric Tavern restaurant, one of Miles' regular haunts next to Waverley station, we first make small talk, finding out a little about each other, when out of the blue, he offers me the job. Without hesitating, I accept, but tell him I want to make two things clear before he accepts my acceptance. Firstly, I have certain issues with stage fright and secondly, I'm not prepared to visit South Africa as long as an apartheid system remains in place.

'Don't worry about that, we can easily sort that out,' is his sympathetic reply to my admission of suffering from a degree of platform nerves and he is equally reassuring about my views on South Africa, saying he has similar concerns and that neither point is a problem.

Done and dusted, all in a few days. Thank you, Heather.

At the same time as being overjoyed at my good fortune and the prospect of my next challenge, I had the same emotional reaction to leaving Newcastle and the Northern Sinfonia as when I left Bergen. Sadness at leaving a place and job I was more than happy with, in exchange for the unknown. I had made so many good friends, taken part in music-making at its most rewarding and given performances of the highest quality with soloists and conductors from the top-drawer. My life was as enjoyable as I could imagine it to be.

I had learned a great deal from being part of that harmonious ensemble, not only as a musician, but also as the orchestra's representative of the Musicians' Union.

All regional orchestras have a Union representative, who among other things, collects membership fees, keeps an eye out for infringements of Union rules and if called upon, arbitrates between players and management. During my stint as an MU steward, the Standard Orchestra contract was radically overhauled. Stewards from each of the regional orchestras met in London on numerous occasions and together with the General Secretary and the Assistant Secretary, hammered out a much-improved contract containing a number of innovations, such as payment for travel time, late-night-return payments and the inclusion of time spent travelling to and from concert venues in the total number of hours worked per week. Finally, although a limited weekly tally of hours was nothing new, a four-weekly tally of hours was. This was agreed and resulted in overtime payments if the number of hours exceeded a stipulated maximum.

For the first time in my life, I felt I had done something practical, however small to justify my political principles.

THIRTEEN

Making friends in a new place is vitally important.
You could do worse than frequent the nearest pub.
Regularly.

My first six weeks in the Edinburgh Quartet were commuting weeks, with weekends spent in Newcastle and weekdays spent lodging with a family in Ann Street in Edinburgh's New Town.

The Ann Street accommodation was a great introduction to the city which was about to become my new home and the weekly commute was far from onerous. The drive between the two cities, through the lush green and undulating scenery of the Borders, on the winding, traffic-free roads of the A68 and A697 was the perfect antidote to the intensity of those first few weeks, offsetting much of the accumulated stress.

The house in Ann Street was owned by Tom and Elizabeth Burns. Tom was Professor of Sociology at Edinburgh University and his wife Elizabeth was also a sociologist and author. In this imposing house on one of the most attractive streets in Edinburgh, these two gently stimulating characters had brought up five children and through one of the daughters who was dating a colleague of mine in the Northern Sinfonia, I found myself temporarily staying there.

The house was always full of warmth, with members of the family coming and going continuously. I was never quite sure who was still living at home or elsewhere and sometimes I was invited to join them for their evening meal, which was always a sparky affair and great fun.

I remember one conversation during an evening meal, when almost all the family were present. It revolved round the film 'Shampoo', starring Warren Beatty as a sex-addicted hairdresser. Words like *wanking* were bandied about unselfconsciously in what ultimately turned out to be a free-flowing discussion on sexual behaviour. I don't remember being unduly embarrassed, but I do remember thinking that such a conversation with my parents, or any of my friends' parents was unimaginable, let alone in the company of three young women I hardly knew. Even though I was twenty-nine years old at the time, the frank and open discussion was a revelation to me on how a difficult topic could be talked about with honesty and good humour, without a flicker of awkwardness.

I also remember Elizabeth's novel alternative to owning an expensive pressure cooker. She simply placed a house brick on the lid of a standard saucepan when the need arose. It made quite an amusing sight, seeing one or more saucepans sitting on the Aga, with bricks precariously balanced on their lids.

Staying in Edinburgh for those first few weeks and not knowing anyone was a fairly solitary existence. I felt I could only impose on the Burns' generosity to a limited extent, not because they weren't wholly welcoming, but in order to respect their privacy. At each day's end, rehearsals over and individual practice done back in Ann Street, I, more often than not, headed for one of Edinburgh's plentiful watering holes in the excellent, pub-rich district of Stockbridge, only a stone's throw from my lodgings. St. Stephen Street in particular offered a fine selection of bars, from The Bailie at one end, to St Vincent Bar at the other. The St Vincent soon became a regular haunt of mine. I liked its three-step descent from the street and its plentiful and unusual use of light-coloured wood in the bar. It was also a little quieter than most bars which suited my close-of-day moods.

Friday nights however were never quiet and on one particular Friday, the St. Vincent was overflowing. Once inside and with a pint of Deuchars safely in my hand, I fought my way to the only available seat and perched myself on the end of an already overcrowded bench. Squashed up beside me was a group of friends in their early twenties and in front of us, a narrow table supporting a large collection of glasses in various stages of fullness. The collector in chief of empty glasses was a rather doddery old woman whose sense of balance was being sorely tested by the jostling clientele who filled every available standing space. By the time she arrived at our table, she was looking decidedly unsteady and a timely nudge from the assembled melee caused her to lose balance. In an attempt to steady herself, she abruptly extended a hand through the seething crowd to reach for our table and in the process knocked over our glasses, spilling the contents into the laps of me and my neighbours.

The Edinburgh Quartet outside St. Mark's Church,
Edinburgh, 1975

Helen, the glass-gatherer was unhurt and things returned to normal once the floor was mopped and the empty glasses replenished. The only evidence of the incident that remained was our damp clothes and undamped demeanour, which together, removed any inhibitions we might have had and we slipped naturally into conversation. These six students were more than happy to chat, doing so until closing time and on the street outside, instead of saying farewell, they invited me back to their flat on Howe Street for further refreshment and we set off towards the centre of town up the steep incline of St.Vincent Street.

Getting close to midnight and after a little more alcohol and a shared spliff, one of the students, a medic called Dick, threw out the idea that tomorrow, after a short night's sleep, we should go for a run. 'There's some kind of relay race taking place on the outskirts of Edinburgh needing a team of four; anyone interested?' This was delivered in his distinct London accent.

This was not met with the degree of enthusiasm Dick had hoped for, so he followed up the query with some necessary cajoling which did have the desired effect. Myself and another medic called Peter signed up and someone referred to as Hoppy made up the numbers. Hoppy was not a resident but a visitor friend of yet another medic called Peter who lived in the flat and who, with his strong Northern Irish accent, was always referred to as Prod to distinguish him from the other Peter (my arrival was not helping things). The completion of the team's personnel now brought the night's carousing to an end and I headed back to Ann Street for a short night's sleep.

In the morning we met outside the Howe Street flat and set off for Craigmillar and the Jack Kane Centre. On the way, we pestered Dick for more details on what we had signed up for, but he was loath to give anything away. It became clear why once we arrived. Today was the annual Scottish Cross-Country Relay Championships.

Dick does a bit of running and is pretty fit; I do a good deal less running, smoke and am far from fit; Peter doesn't run at all but is reasonably fit; Hoppy would be hard-pressed to know what running is, is overweight and unfit and turns up in attire for the run which looks more suitable for Portobello beach on a summer's day than for a four kilometre leg of a sixteen-kilometre run.

Dick takes on the first leg in commendable fashion, handing over to me with a reasonable number of competitors still behind us. Despite my best effort, at the end of my lap with only half the course completed, I'm a couple of hundred metres adrift of the rest of the field as I hand over to beachcomber Hoppy under the concerned gaze of the officiating race marshals. Before Hoppy comes into sight at the end of his circuit, several teams have already completed the race and the disgruntled officials try to encourage the hapless Peter to abandon his leg, as it's apparent that our team is now so far behind the rest of the field that they will have to devote an extra half-hour marshalling the course, solely to accommodate us.

What was that about the hare and the tortoise? Peter ploughs on, honour is at stake. . .

The marshals are livid as he finally brings our team home. Their anger, combined with our embarrassment ensures we exit more rapidly from the scene, moving faster than at any other time that day.

The episode was far from the disaster it appeared, as the friendship struck up in St. Vincent Bar the night before was securely cemented by the momentous lack of success we shared on the playing fields of Scotland. From that time and through that friendship, many more friends have been made, all of whom I would never have met without the intervention of the tottering Helen. Lots of medics of course, but not exclusively: forty-five years later I'm still in touch with all of them and some have become really close friends.

FOURTEEN

An orchestral violinist is expected to obey, shut up and play. In a string quartet everyone is an individual with a solo musical line to himself – and a voice!

My first Edinburgh Quartet rehearsal in August 1975 moved me into an entirely different world, not just a change of location to the incomparably beautiful city of Edinburgh, a city constantly nudging you with its history and architectural delights, but also a change of role within a musical group.

The role of an orchestral violinist is very much akin to a willing school pupil: turn up on time, sit quietly and attentively for six hours a day and do exactly as directed by the teacher/conductor. Rank-and-file players are neither expected nor encouraged to have a say in the workings of a rehearsal, a situation which on rare occasions can result in some peculiar behaviour. A normally placid sub-principal violin in the Northern Sinfonia became so enraged by the principal conductor's demeanour during a rehearsal that he completely lost it, launched himself at speed from his seat and with violin in one hand and conductor's throat in the other, threatened to throttle him on the spot.

The only real opportunity for a rank-and-file player to influence the functioning of an orchestra is through infrequent orchestral meetings, where players voice their opinions on any number of issues and then, through the orchestral committee, have them presented to the management. I imagine this is much like any business consisting of employers and employees.

In a string quartet consisting of two violins, one viola and one cello, everyone is an individual with a solo musical line to himself – and a voice. I was now able to give vent to anything, from my opinion on all things musical, like tempi, phrasing, balance, lengths of notes to the more practical matters of rehearsal times, programme planning, fees, promotional strategy and so on.

Finding novel ways of advertising concerts was one of the more frivolous ways I played around with this freedom. In the early days of ever-present graffiti, there was a time when everywhere you looked, the letters OK would be added to a single word, like a kind of suffix. Trying to be trendy, I placed an advert for one of our concerts which featured Bartok, using the heading Bart-OK!

I did get into hot water over another advert I placed which was to drum up an audience for the Brazilian composer Villa-Lobos – *JULIAN BREAM* doesn't have a monopoly on the music of Villa-Lobos, come and hear etc.

We did receive a couple of letters accusing us of misleading information. . .

School's out. I now had a job where I was fortunate enough to have direct influence on every aspect of our work and take responsibility for all decisions made in collaboration with my three colleagues. In effect, a co-operative.

We did of course have help in running the Quartet, usually one person, paid part-time and another on a voluntary basis. Early in my twenty-three years as a member of the EQ, we were making plans for a tour to Yugoslavia. You probably know that at that time Yugoslavia was known as the Socialist Federal Republic of Yugoslavia with a communist government; it was a composite of the five countries that now exist in its place, Croatia and Serbia being the two largest. Sharing his time and expertise voluntarily and helping us in any way he could in this was the indispensable Bert Davis, a retired British Council Director of which Yugoslavia had been one of his postings.

Bert stood no more than five feet, four inches tall, dapper and with a personality that compensated for his diminutive stature. His energy at the age of eighty was remarkable and his joy of life infectious. This enthusiasm for life was particularly well displayed by his interest in all aspects of the Arts which he shared with Margaret, his ever-present companion of several decades. His wife and daughter, safely tucked away at home appeared to take this arrangement calmly in their stride. Incidentally, he was in the same tank corps during World War Two as the renowned Gaelic poet Sorley McLean and their friendship sustained until Sorley's death in 1996.

On Bert's suggestion, along with his highly flattering recommendation, we approached the British Council asking for its support in this venture. The result was hopeful and some weeks later, bigwigs from the British Council in London were despatched to Edinburgh to listen to us play, discuss our proposed trip and with a bit of luck, put their financial seal on the trip.

The EQ is affiliated to Edinburgh University, so we chose to meet in St. Cecilia's Hall, part of a building which houses the University's Raymond Russell Collection of Early Keyboard Instruments. We thought the small and impressive concert hall would be a suitable space for beguiling the representatives into providing the requisite support.

St. Cecilia's Hall is situated in a less than glamorous part of the city called the Cowgate, deep in the bowels of the Old Town, an area familiar to me for two other reasons besides the university connection. I'm a 'Real Ale' enthusiast and pubs that sold real ale were few and far between in the 1970s and I knew all of them in Edinburgh. As I was now living in Clarence Street, Clark's Bar, an unpretentious, local establishment at the bottom of Dundas Street became the hub for my socialising. A place where dedicated drinking companions and I spent far too much time with our fists wrapped around a straight glass of Deuchars IPA, engaged in wide-ranging banter. We did make excursions to many of the others and one of them, the Green Tree happened to be a mere 150 yards from St. Cecilia's Hall. After Clark's, the Green Tree was the next most patronised watering hole due to its proximity to the workplace of three of my drinking companions; it also had a convenient opening time of one hour earlier than Clark's.

The second reason for the area's familiarity was almost the antithesis of the first. One evening a week I did voluntary work at the Peoples Palace, not a pub, but a night shelter for the homeless, tucked up a close just off the Cowgate and run by the Church of Scotland. It offered a basic but secure environment, providing a little nourishment and a place to lay your head. As volunteers, we dished out soup and bread when the doors opened at 10 pm and supervised those staying the night by handing out old newspapers and offering help to anyone looking for a portion of floor to sleep on that was to their liking. As the food was consumed and the hall filled, we tried to have a sympathetic and calming influence on an extremely volatile group in varying degrees of intoxication, depression and the many other mental and physical conditions that had led to their sorry plight.

It was a large room devoid of furniture and the unfortunate residents slept directly on the wooden floor of this typical church hall. The newspapers were by way of bedding and served as a kind of concession to hygiene by providing, however insubstantial, a barrier between body and floor. Many of those who frequented the Peoples Palace were alcoholics, with confrontation and conflict ever present, usually over personal space and minor irritations easily escalated into physical altercations. Their inability to cope with life's many adversities was more than enough reason to lose control in most cases.

I got to know the regulars as time went by and I learnt

the names of most if not all, as they remembered mine.

The day of the British Council meeting arrived and we all gathered in St. Cecilia's Hall at ten in the morning. Having made our introductions, the British Council contingent then settled into their seats and the Quartet proceeded with their charm offensive by performing a couple of sample pieces, one of which was by Kenneth Leighton, the Reid Professor of Music at the university. His Severn Variations for string quartet is a little gem and one which often strikes a chord with audiences. On the strength of a broadcast performance of the Leighton on Radio 3, we once secured a date at the Lichfield Festival which had been heard by the then director of the festival who was recovering at home after a serious operation.

After an hour, a break was suggested and we headed along the Cowgate in search of a coffee bar. I was leading our small entourage along the narrow pavement, when in the distance I spied three of my regulars from the People's Palace coming towards us. They were definitely not sober and were supporting each other, arms draped over shoulders, bottles in hand and staggering ever closer. As we were about to pass, they look up,

'Pee'a, hoo ya doin son?'

'Hi Billy, I'm fine. How are you lot?' I stop for a chat while my colleagues briefly hesitate, long enough to take in the scene before continuing without me.

'No bad son, no bad. Where ye goin?'

'Oh, we're just looking for somewhere to have a coffee.'

'Good on ye, good on ye son.' The conversation drifted

on in a similar vein and by the time we said our farewells, the St. Cecilia group were disappearing into the distance. I soon caught them up and almost immediately, we find a café.

I was expecting curiosity to get the better of everyone once the coffee arrived and we were settled at a table and I was ready and prepared to fend off any caustic remarks. Nothing. Not one person made mention of what had just taken place, neither the BC representatives nor my colleagues. I was really surprised but also quite impressed that their lack of curiosity might have indicated that better nature had triumphed over self-satisfied smugness, or even disgust.

I decided to stay stum as well: it amused me to think that by not offering an explanation, the chance encounter was left hanging, enigmatically in the air. I am also happy to report that the incident had no deleterious effect on the day's business and the tour went ahead with full and gratefully received support from the British Council.

St. Cecilia's Hall had another noteworthy connection for the Quartet. It came about as a result of political turmoil that existed between the USSR and the West during the Cold War years, which had ramifications in both the sporting world and the world of culture.

In 1983, the then Professor of Defence Studies at the University of Edinburgh, the eminent academic and writer, John Erickson, initiated a yearly series of informal discussions between prominent political figures from the West and their counterparts in the Soviet Union. These were known as the *Edinburgh Conversations* and took place on alternate years in Edinburgh and Moscow.

Since the invasion of Afghanistan by the Soviet Union in 1979, the United Kingdom had suspended diplomatic relations with the Soviets. Cultural exchanges had all but petered out and sporting events were boycotted, leading to sixty-six countries refusing to participate in the Moscow Olympic Games in 1980. These *Conversations* amounted to about the only conspicuous communication between the two antagonists and ran until 1988. They were informal and intended to be of a conciliatory nature, conducted in a relaxed manner, face to face in a neutral setting. In Edinburgh, they took place in St. Cecilia's Hall.

The numbers for these intimate gatherings were small, six or seven individuals only and on two occasions in Edinburgh the Conversations culminated in a performance by the EQ, followed by dinner to which we were also invited. I remember feeling well out of my depth on one occasion when sitting at the same table as the editor of *Pravda*, Victor Afanasyev, but at the same time, feeling extremely privileged at being in on a little bit of history in the making, the aims of which fitted comfortably with my own political views.

The only political opinion I dared share with the assembled cognoscenti was non vocal. I simply had on display on the lapel of my dinner jacket, my CND badge.

For me, Edinburgh's Cowgate will for ever be associated as the place where the world was put to rights, whether it was among my close friends over the consumption of copious amounts of real ale in the Green Tree, in particular Charles

Wild and Eddie Harper, or through the lessons learned from my time helping out at the People's Palace, or finally my part in bringing about the end of the Cold War through the Conversations and facilitating the restoration of democracy in the East, practically single-handed.

FIFTEEN

Post-concert socialising with hosts can be tiresome involving a barrage of predictable questions. But appearances can be deceptive on an Olympian scale.

My twenty-three years as a member of the Edinburgh Quartet was the most substantial period of my career and the most rewarding. Membership afforded me a way of life I could otherwise only have ever dreamt of. I loved the playing part of it and everything else fitted around it perfectly, with plenty of time for family, leisure, social activities and much else besides.

Playing was not limited to the Quartet either; as an individual, I frequently deputised in both the Scottish Chamber Orchestra and the Scottish Baroque Ensemble and the Quartet was regularly invited to swell the ranks of the Scottish Radio Orchestra, (no longer in existence) as well as lead the string sections in an *ad hoc* orchestra at Scottish Television for numerous light-music shows, providing the backing for the likes of Hogmanay and Burns celebrations with Andy Stewart, Kenneth McKellar and Moira Anderson. 'Highway' with Harry Secombe was a regular little earner too. All far removed from the rarefied world of string quartets.

The variety was most welcome, likewise the remuneration it provided and the Quartet's regular touring punctuated each year's mostly domestic work, introducing new experiences and keeping things fresh.

A tour in the 1980s took us on a second trip to Canada. The first had been to Toronto and the Great Lakes, which for me was memorable for only one reason. I spent the whole tour when not playing, lying on my back even when travelling in our hired van. My recurring back problem had flared up shortly before leaving and was so painful, the prone position was the only means of gaining any relief.

I was in much better shape for this 1980 tour to the West, in the Vancouver and British Columbia area, with a brief excursion across the US border for a single concert in Seattle.

The largest portion of our work came from playing for Music Clubs, both at home and abroad. These clubs operate on very tight budgets and rely on financial support from national and regional arts funding organisations and the goodwill of local businesses. But most important of all, the clubs are operated by volunteers without whom they would not exist. Through their selfless generosity, both in time and in practical matters, these clubs flourish around the world.

A pocket-sized string quartet is a far more mobile musical unit than an orchestra and doesn't necessarily need hotel accommodation when touring. To save money, these hard-pressed clubs jump at the chance to save on hotel expenses, which otherwise would substantially increase the Quartet's fee and run the risk of us losing the engagement altogether. So, more often than not, they are prepared to provide accommodation from among their willing and able members.

The benefits and drawbacks of this arrangement can be numerous and sometimes it is difficult to know which party benefits or loses out the most. The total booking package can be contingent upon these arrangements and the Quartet tends to readily accept whatever is provided, however luxurious or bizarre. Lack of privacy, supply of food and sharing rooms are examples where less than satisfactory provision might well occur.

By far the most tiresome part of these home-accommodation situations can be the repetitive nature of questions from enthusiastic and interested hosts. Post-concert socialising could often mean a snack and drink, or sometimes a full-blown meal back at your host's house, whilst facing a barrage of predictable questions about our lives as musicians. A late night was inevitable.

If two or more of us were billeted together, one of us was sometimes able to escape the interrogation under the camouflage of some barely believable excuse. This worked as an acceptable compromise and ensured that at least one of us got to bed at a reasonable time.

This situation, repeated night after night could take its toll. Yet. . . it was not always so. Not far north of Vancouver in British Columbia, we are giving an afternoon concert in an ecologically impressive Native American lodge, built entirely from huge tree trunks and fronted by a highly decorated

Totem Pole. After the concert, we have been told that we will be met by one of our hosts, who will guide us to where we will be staying for the next two nights. Hilda and Maynard are the names of our hosts and they will be providing accommodation for the whole Quartet. Only Hilda will be at the concert and it's her station wagon we will follow back to their house.

Just before the concert, Hilda is pointed out to us as she walks from the car park and my heart sinks at the sight of this dowdily dressed woman in her sixties. From her appearance, I instantly conjure up a depressing mental picture of how the next two days are going to pan out. She is wearing a non-descript grey ankle length raincoat and a 1950s vintage brown cloche-type hat under which straggly unkempt strands of her hair are making random appearances. A pair of dated, slightly skewwhiff horn-rimmed glasses sit upon her nose and shabby shoes cover her feet: her emphatic gait does however, come as a welcome redeeming feature.

After the concert, Hilda introduces herself and we all say our farewells to the local organisers. Hilda chats a little, mentioning a few things about the journey ahead and then matter-of-factly points out which vehicle is hers. She comes across as friendly but unremarkable.

I'm in low spirits as we pile into our van and prepare to follow Hilda's station wagon, resigned to expecting the worst. I fear the approaching well-earned couple of free days will be the predictable round of questions and boring time-filling entertainment. After a journey lasting at least an hour, our destination comes into view. The clapboard house is large and impressive, full of character, set in substantial grounds on a peninsula with gardens sloping down to water which must be an inlet from the sea; a sight which instantly begins to disperse the dark cloud hanging over me.

'Velcome to Quadra Island' is the loud greeting from Maynard, standing on the front steps of the house. This shambolic and voluble émigré Dutchman is already at 5.30 in the afternoon, showing obvious signs of inebriation. My suspicions are confirmed, when before we have unloaded our suitcases and been properly introduced, he suggests we join him in a glass of homemade vodka, astonishingly made from peas. The sensible suggestion is pounced upon with alacrity, with Hilda more than happy to join us in a pre-prandial drink and looking noticeably more comfortable now she is at home with glass in hand.

My ill-founded preconceptions are looking decidedly misguided right now. There are other people wandering in and out of this friendly house. On occasion we are introduced to a passer-by if they linger long enough; they seem to be neighbours, although a lone Frenchman is a resident, renting a shack in the garden by the water's edge, fifty metres from the house. He is eccentric to say the least, spending his summers playing chess alone in the garden, in the buff.

This surprising household is gradually revealing its true colours, like a butterfly freeing itself from its pupa. The whereabouts of our sleeping quarters is still not fully known. Miles and Chris know they are staying in the main house and as dusk is now setting in, Michael and I are given torches and directed to a small log cabin in a remote spot in the garden.

We lug our heavy suitcases across a rough lawn and open the door to our temporary living quarters. We enter a small square room where a log burning stove is providing heat and filling the room with a warm orange glow. There is only this one room, but from its centre, a rudimentary ladder rises to a platform with a couple of mattresses on the floor, indicating our sleeping quarters. This unexpected arrangement is certainly unusual, but one that fits snuggly with the unfolding narrative.

Back at the house, Maynard recommends that as it's now low tide, the Frenchman and myself should harvest a few oysters from the readily available source of the seashore at the bottom of the garden, so buckets in hand, we do his bidding. We are rewarded with relatively few, but enough to have made it worthwhile. These are hastily prepared in the kitchen by two more people I have not seen before and with the help of a splash of Tabasco, the oysters are soon despatched to whoever happens to be around.

Alcohol is plentiful with no danger of running out and a wide variety of food starts appearing. Platters piled high like a mobile buffet pass through, generously and continually replenished, easily keeping pace with the unlimited booze.

Hilda (who is also Dutch) and Maynard tell us that they moved to Quadra Island from Holland over forty years ago and were just about the only inhabitants. The now, not-so-dowdy Hilda provides the biggest surprise of the evening when she tells us she had been an international athlete, having represented the Netherlands as a rower in more than one Olympic Games in the forties and fifties.

I've always believed that preconceptions based on

people's appearance is a mistake and to have ignored this tenet when observing Hilda for the first time, makes me feel extremely weak and foolish. It never becomes completely clear how Maynard has passed these last forty years. Reading between the lines, I have an inkling that he could have been a lawyer, or perhaps has just had his fingers in lots of different pies, but now in retirement he is without doubt living life to the full. He is obsessed by the British Royal Family. Perched on a picture rail in the living room is a miniature replica of the coronation coach and horses which he seems inordinately proud of.

More people briefly pass by, including another neighbour and her boyfriend, who is in training for the *Iron Man* triathlon in Hawaii in two weeks' time – no pea vodka for him. I recognise no one from the concert the night before and music is not a prominent topic of conversation for a change, which comes as a blessing.

A certain amount of sweet-smelling smoke is hanging in the air but it's not cigarette smoke and it's a bit too pungent to be coming from the stove. One look at Maynard clears up the mystery. He's puffing away on a spliff, offering it to anyone interested in a drag. I can say with great certainty that this is not Maynard's first spliff, or his last.

Children with long teeth keep appearing at the door, dressed in garish clothes, cloaks and pointed hats and demanding sweets. Until this moment, I have been completely unaware that tonight, adding to the general air of unreality, is Halloween.

One of the most entertaining evenings of my life continues

into the late hours in the same surreal vein and by the time bedtime arrives, I'm exhausted. It's been a long day, one full of variety and wonderful surprises. I can't wait to be lulled to sleep wrapped in warm thoughts, surrounded by an orange glow.

The next morning I'm up early because Hilda wants to show me around the small island. Over their forty years here, they have carved out tracks in the surrounding hills by cutting back dense foliage and coppicing or removing trees. They have made the tracks even more accessible by using some of the felled logs to strengthen and prop up steep-sided banks and build steps where necessary. It's been a huge undertaking over a prolonged period with remarkable results. They continue the maintenance of this large acreage, personalising it with unofficial signposts and names for all the tracks.

The remainder of the day is a little more orthodox than yesterday. We are invited to roam around the house and surrounding area at our leisure and to feel free to do whatever takes our fancy. A few of their friends join us in the evening for a meal and the day peters out comfortably and naturally.

Our time with Hilda and Maynard draws to an end and the following morning we sadly take our leave. I say goodbye to two people who have made an indelible impression and with whom I shall stay in touch.

Another billet in British Columbia, much further north, was remarkable for a different reason. In the township of Prince Rupert 1500 km north of Vancouver, I was farmed out for the night to an émigré Scottish couple. He was a doctor and his wife a nurse and in our post-concert chat back at their house, our first chance to relax in each other's company revealed we had more in common than we realised.

My hosts both trained and met in Edinburgh and during their courtship my hostess often used to babysit the children of her husband's Professor at his house in Bonnington Grove, Edinburgh. Not surprisingly, both she and I were able to describe the layout of this house in detail, as Professor Carswell had been the previous owner of the very same house that was at that time my family home.

SIXTEEN

Don't be averse to encroaching on another branch of entertainment: the Edinburgh Quartet joins the ranks of famous Italian sporting heroes.

At the age of thirty-five and within the space of one month, my life underwent four life-changing events: the birth of Polly, my second child; becoming vegetarian (lasting two years) quitting smoking (after twenty years); and taking up running as a regular pastime.

The smoking was finally exorcised with the help of Nicorette chewing gum, the gum accomplishing in a mere ten days what the previous five years of willpower had failed to do. Being conscious of the blasphemy of downing pints of Deuchar's in Clark's Bar whilst chewing gum at the same time, must have also added to the speed of my exorcism.

Running soon turned into a passion and returning to it, having had no more than sporadic jogs around Edinburgh's Inverleith Park since my schooldays, was cathartic as well as a major help in boosting my resolve. (I had been a bit of an athlete at school, a member of the rugby, cricket and athletic teams and captain of the gym and cross-country teams, accomplishing second place in the under fourteen's East London Cross-Country Championships.)

On one of our trips to Italy, the Quartet had been provided with accommodation to cover our four-day stay in the northern city of Varese. The hotel was modern and practical, but soulless. My room had a single window reminiscent of one you might find in a medieval castle, with an aperture so mean it struggled to let in the most meagre amount of light. Covering the floor was a thin, felt-like luminous green carpet so completely unforgiving that it must have been fitted without underlay, straight on to concrete. Dreadful! I was not going to spend four days entombed in this dark room, so I went in search of alternative lodgings.

Close to the hotel, I soon found a sports bar advertising rooms. I ventured inside the dimly lit bar which looked as though it had not been renovated since last century and as I approached the counter through the gloom, I could see that an attempt had been made to lift the room's murkiness by lining the walls with photos of famous Italian sports personalities. These greatly outnumbered the handful of customers huddled beneath them, who also appeared in need of renovation. The barman was friendly if a little dour but spoke enough English to understand my enquiry about a room. It turned out he was also the owner and immediately took me upstairs to appraise what he had on offer, with no concerns about leaving his bar unattended. I was buoyed up the moment he opened the door to the first room. Sunlight was streaming through an enormous window onto a floor that was no less unforgiving than what I had just left, only this one was the real deal of highly decorated ceramic tiles consistent with the age of the building. Things got even better on discovering the window of this first-floor room opened onto a balcony with a view over orange-coloured pantile rooftops to the hills beyond. It was exactly what I was looking for and I was happy to free up my state-of-the-art accommodation for a more appreciative guest.

Back in the bar, we put a seal on the transaction by agreeing a price which I'm sure he just plucked out of the air. I had no qualms about incurring this extra expense as the figure he suggested was so ludicrously low.

Whenever I was on tour, I always made sure I had enough space in my suitcase to tuck away my running gear and like the more memorable performances we have given, various runs in locations around the world are etched in my memory.

Each day in Varese, I practised in my room followed by a run. My routine was well observed as I knew my violin playing could be heard in the bar and my only route to the street was through the bar. My presence was beginning to cause a bit of a stir. Through snippets of conversation with the proprietor, he now knew what I was doing in Varese and consequently so did his customers. His interest led him to ask for a photo of the Quartet, to which I duly obliged. The day after receiving the photo, he handed it back, not through any dissatisfaction but with a request for it to be autographed by each member of the Quartet.

On my final day, I went for a long run to the top of Monte San Giorgio, about eighteen miles in total and on my way, I passed a group of school children who stopped and applauded me as I wheezed past. My first thought was that they had mistaken me for someone else, but soon realised they were just being flamboyantly Italian.

Back at the bar, I met with another round of applause – that's if you can consider the noise emanating from only four or five people a round – because on the wall alongside the bar's collection of Italian sporting heroes, was hanging the newly framed photo of the Edinburgh Quartet. That should confuse a few customers.

The runs of memorable significance when on the road with the Edinburgh Quartet were numerous. Setting out on a run from my hotel in Kuwait City, I discovered that the building next door but one was the American Embassy. On each corner of the fortress-like embassy was a tower, mounted by a machine gun post and as I approached on the public footpath, the guard in the nearest tower swung his machine gun round, pointing it in my direction and commanded in bellicose tones for me to go no further, cross to the pavement on the other side of the road and continue from there.

A little scary and possibly a step or two out of the embassy's jurisdiction, even though this occurred in the aftermath of Iraq's invasion of Kuwait in 1990. I did comply.

In Abu Dhabi I thought I was in with a chance to win a car. The five-kilometre race, out and back along the promenade was so badly organised, that I think, like the Korean war, it probably still hasn't officially finished. The road along the Promenade had been closed to traffic for the day, providing a route with enough space to accommodate both runners and free-ranging spectators. Everything started well as the small field of runners set off, encouraged by the thousands of curious onlookers. At the halfway point I was doing alright and now heading back in the direction from which I had come, my confidence was quietly building. I was possibly in tenth place, feeling good and in contact with those in front of me.

I picked off a couple more competitors as we entered the final two kilometres and was beginning to look forward in true Chariots of Fire fashion, to a podium finish, maybe winning. I was even allowing myself to indulge in the fantasy of driving back to Scotland in my newly won Cadillac, when suddenly, we hurtled headlong into the general public coming in the opposite direction.

The spectators that saw us off, obviously thought the race would end in an entirely different location, not realising that the planned route would bring us back along the promenade, finishing where we started. They were now taking full advantage of the traffic-free prom. Nonchalant groups in holiday mood were strewn out in every direction, creating an impenetrable mass of bodies. Running was no longer an option: trying to walk in a straight line through dense thicket would have been easier.

I never made it to the finish line and later heard that the end of the race was so shambolic, that the whole event was re-scheduled for the following week. Little use to me as by then I would be in another part of the desert, the Cadillac having slipped through my fingers like sand.

Driving to venues in a Cadillac would have been an eye-

Dumfries marathon, 1986

catching and novel way to travel around Scotland, but we contented ourselves on continuing to rely mostly, upon my dependable old Saab 9000. I did most of the driving, sharing it with Michael. Miles couldn't drive, Chris was not interested and Mark, Chris's replacement as cellist in 1985 did drive, but so badly, we didn't let him. I suspected that Mark was self-taught through watching too many car chases in silent movies. His perambulating fared little better, one moment he would be walking in a perfectly executed straight line, the next might find him with one foot in the road, having suddenly shot off at an oblique angle for no apparent reason. If there was an equivalent of the DVLA driving test for walking, he would be very unlikely to have passed. He was a definite danger to motorists in more ways than one.

Mark joined the quartet after an hiatus of only six months without a permanent cellist, narrowly pipping Kevin McCrea, a local cellist in the Scottish Chamber Orchestra to the post. He came to us from a small chamber group based in Peterborough and at the age of twenty-six was the youngest member of the quartet by at least a decade and amazingly, as I write this, he still occupies that position thirty-eight years later.

During my time in the EQ, we visited most of the many inhabited lands off the Scottish coast: Arran, Islay, Skye, the Western Isles, both Inner and Outer, Orkney, Shetland and many more and only once did we fall prey to the vagaries of Atlantic weather systems. This is made all the more remarkable because our visits to the most remote islands always took place in the depths of winter.

Linaclate Community Centre on the Outer Hebridean island of Benbecula was one of our regular venues and that is where we found ourselves when our schedule was abruptly rewritten by the ferocious winds of an Atlantic storm. We had completed our musical obligations on the island with an afternoon children's concert, followed by a public concert in the evening and were making the short car journey back to our accommodation for the night, when we became very aware of a distinct change in the weather. The following morning, we were expecting to catch the Caledonian MacBrayne ferry from Lochmaddy on North Uist, well known for its vulnerability to extreme weather conditions.

By bedtime, the adverse weather conditions were giving rise to rumours that there was a real possibility of disruption to the Lochmaddy sailing in the morning. As I went to bed, the wind had already built to a level where it could be clearly heard swirling and bouncing off the less structurally sound areas of the hotel's exterior.

I was woken in the morning by the sound of the wind raging against my window and funnelling its voice through any willing aperture it could find. A full-scale storm was underway, pinning us down in this most basic of hotels and shutting down our only escape route. The turbulent sea pummelling the Lochmaddy pier made it impossible for the ferry to dock and we were now at the mercy of the wind, which alone would decide at what point a departure would be possible. We just had to make the best of it until the storm blew itself out.

Looking back, I don't remember us rehearsing to fill the

time, which was rather strange. I can only imagine that in constant hope of an imminent departure, we felt that setting up and getting stuck into a three-hour rehearsal would be too readily an admission of acceptance of the situation. Musical scales were in less need of scrutiny than the Beaufort scale just then.

The time dragged on and by the second day of incarceration, I thought a run would be the ideal antidote to confinement. The temperature wasn't bad enough to deter me, but the ominous sound of the wind howling and whistling round the building was a tad alarming. A look out of the window at the coarse ground vegetation being buffeted about like the jangled nerves of someone in the midst of an apoplectic fit, did nothing to allay my apprehension.

I had never experienced winds of such strength. I ventured outside, fighting my way out of the door and on to the road. I then tried running into the wind but couldn't. I felt sure the alternative of running with the wind would have resulted in being slammed into the tarmac. I tried walking but couldn't. It was all I could do to stay on my feet. The shortest run of my life but one of the best remembered came to an end as I stumbled with the aid of a fence as a handrail back through the hotel door. I then unexpectantly burst into laughter for much the same reason I did about five minutes into Concerto Grosso No 1 by Alfred Schnittke when hearing it for the first time. The effect of a truly mind-boggling and immediate contrast.

Ronnie Birks, 2nd violin in the Lindsays, the violinist I replaced in the Northern Sinfonia, was also a keen runner.

Maybe it's a 2nd violin thing. It has been suggested that the voice of reason within a string Quartet often presides at that chair, so what better way of ensuring the ability to reason stays in decent shape, than keeping fit?

The Lindsays and the Edinburgh Quartet shared a gig, playing at the same festival on consecutive days in Provence in 1996. Both Quartets were staying at the same hotel and our rehearsal schedules worked out in such a way that Ronnie and I were free at the same time one afternoon. I think I had seen Ronnie once and only briefly, since 1975, so the obvious celebration for our reunion was a run together.

When I arrived at his room as arranged, he was still polishing off his lunch of a few grapes, a selection of nuts, some cheese and a roll. It was almost identical to the sort of meal I might eat when on tour, but I would definitely have added a few tomatoes.

During our run on this free spring afternoon, we had a fascinating chat, as we padded around the aromatic Provencal countryside. We had a general catch-up on the twenty years since last spending any time together and compared thoughts on life as 2nd violin in our respective quartets. Relationships within the quartets and how the differing personalities affected the way rehearsals operated inevitably dominated the conversation, with a few anecdotes thrown in at the expense of our colleagues. Coincidentally, Bernie Smith the Lindsays cellist had been one of my closest friends on the Essex Youth Orchestra courses.

I haven't seen Ronnie since, but the small world of music and the internet, means I know what he's up to. *

A race in Baltimore, a local club run in Muscat and a run round the rooftop car park at Toronto airport between flights, are three more runs that come easily to mind. Remembering my runs has been a great marker of when and where I was during that twenty-year period of wallowing in running.

It covered the time from the birth of my two children, through almost the whole of my time in the Edinburgh Quartet and for a few years beyond. Knee injuries eventually brought that sporting activity to an end in 2005.

---

*I have learnt since writing this chapter that Ronnie died in 2020, and I never saw him again after that magical run in Provence.

SEVENTEEN

The line between celebration and indulgence needs careful monitoring. And always think carefully about the best preparations for a handspring!

In 1980, we toured Poland, taking with us an adventurous programme of twentieth century British compositions. The tour was under the auspices of the British Council, which exists primarily for the purpose of building connections between the UK and other countries through arts and culture, education and the English language. Championing British contemporary composers is very much part of that brief and Poland, well known for its avant-garde approach to music, was an obvious choice for such a venture. William Walton's quartet in A minor, the ever-popular Severn Variations by Kenneth Leighton, Thomas Wilson, the American born Scottish composer's 4th quartet written for us in 1976 and in deference to our hosts, a quartet by Andrzej Panufnik were four of the pieces in our repertoire for this tour.

On the other hand, playing music written in the present day will always come with a certain amount of risk for performers and promotors alike. Future engagements can depend on the impression left by a group's visit and as our cellist Chris was wont to say, 'Most of the people that constitute a string quartet audience seem to prefer listening to music written by composers who have completed their lifespan in a terminal fashion,' or words to that effect. Bearing this in mind, one venue on this tour registered higher in the anxiety stakes than any of the others.

Jelenia Gora was an unfamiliar name to me and one of the venues in which we were to perform our exclusively British contemporary music programme. I offered the opinion to our Polish agent/chaperone, that considering the programme we would be playing, the audience will be highly musically literate. Her reply was reassuring and extremely surprising, 'Yes, no need to worry about Jelenia Gora appreciating your concert, it's a mining town.' An image of Les Dawson entertaining a working men's club in Britain flashed across my mind, so it was hard to envisage a room full of miners attentively listening to a string quartet performing Thomas Wilson and Andrzej Panufnik.

She was right though, we even played an encore and several of the audience came backstage, eager to learn more about the composers. We were based in Wroclaw for the tour, staying in a modern utilitarian hotel built in typical socialist style: a solid block of order and straight lines with not a curve in sight. All meals were taken in the hotel's dining room to the accompaniment of its resident music group, a trio of electric keyboard, bass guitar and drum kit and from their functional and glum delivery, I suspect communist ideology along the lines of providing employment and services as part of a production line also had a hand in the formation of this combo.

With not a chance in hell of enhancing the eating experience, it did have the unintentional benefit of distracting the diners from their plates of humdrum food. The perfunctorily played repertoire of a mere four pieces was repeated over and over again until the last customer was driven from the restaurant desperately seeking peace from the musical bludgeoning. Muzak might have been less offensive and have achieved a greater level of human bonding. I can't imagine that what was being provided was entirely in the poor musicians' hands.

The Yugoslavian tour I mentioned earlier, also supported by the British Council, included a two-day residency at a contemporary music festival in Radenci, a spa town in what is now Slovenia. (Radenci mineral water could be bought at the time from Herbie delicatessen in Stockbridge, Edinburgh. Maybe it still can.) The festival was centred in a modern hotel and our commitments were to lunchtime and evening concerts on the first day, finishing with a lunchtime concert the following day.

After the evening performance on the first day, I decided that when the next day's lunchtime concert was over, I would treat myself to an afternoon luxuriating in the hotel's swimming pool, with plenty of alcoholic refreshment as my companion. The three programmes consisting of 20th century works, would include those by Lennox Berkley, Benjamin Britten, Edmund Rubbra and Michael Tippet which I personally found, as with many contemporary compositions, more stressful to perform than the better-known core repertoire. The difficulty arose through a lack of ameliorating components such as familiar phrasing, harmonic structure and regular rhythmical patterns which always helped to overcome any technical and musical problems. This is not to say I didn't enjoy playing twentieth century repertoire. How could I not when faced with playing works by Bartok, Tippet and Britten? The new soundscapes and demanding irregular rhythms were a welcome challenge. So, as an epilogue to the three taxing programmes, I concluded a bit of self-indulgence would be justified. We would also have three free days in Zagreb before our next concert, leaving plenty of time in which to recover if necessary.

The well-earned afternoon arrived and the swimming pool beckoned, a large airy expanse of water enhanced by coloured underwater lighting. The hours drifted by as I splashed and drank my way through the afternoon in a pool I had completely to myself. By early evening, the necessity for food had arrived. Having removed myself from the water and now dressed, I went in search of much needed sustenance in the dining room. Another festival participant was a Yugoslavian pianist, who with his girlfriend, was already having a meal in the dining room. We had met earlier so it was natural enough for me to join them. They both spoke good English, expressing themselves with ease and saying how much they had enjoyed our concerts. The conversation should have been comfortable and relaxed had I not been in the presence of one of the most strikingly beautiful women I had ever seen.

My equilibrium was in danger, as awkwardness and careless attempts to get morsels of food into my mouth and not down my shirt became major obstacles to overcome, although the leisure activities of the afternoon had seen off a degree of inhibition.

By the time the couple came to leave the dining room, the pianist, who was giving that evening's recital, had agreed that after the concert, he and his girlfriend would join myself and the rest of the EQ on the hotel terrace for end of festival celebratory drinks.

With the pianist's recital now over, the six of us gathered as arranged on the terrace and with the aid of further lubrication, chatted away like old friends, until towards the end of the balmy night, my over-imbibing and preoccupation with this very distracting woman led to some eminently bizarre behaviour on my part. In a moment of seeking the limelight, I set about putting on a display of gymnastics on the lawn adjacent to the terrace, from somersaults to head flips and handsprings.

Miraculously, I survived and returned to my seat feeling exceedingly drunk. The action of imitating the motions of a tumble drier, together with my excessive consumption of alcohol finally put paid to any sense of balance I had left, leaving me with no option but to depart rapidly and somehow make it back to my room.

I remember the last leg of the journey along the hotel corridor as being fraught with danger from invisible forces, forces which propelled me from one side of the corridor to the other against my will, until reaching my room. After grappling successfully with the lock to my door, I collapsed on to the bed fully clothed and fell asleep instantly.

The next day brought a different impairment. My restored sense of balance wasn't enough relief to offset the new maladies now attacking my system: headache, nausea, loss of appetite and feelings of detachment from reality. I was barely able to endure the three-hour taxi ride to Zagreb, which was interrupted when the driver of my taxi unaccountably brought it to a halt by slamming on the brakes in an emergency stop. Leaving the now stationary vehicle straddling the busy road, he got out mumbling to himself and went walk-about in the road in front of the car for a good two minutes before getting back in. All this done without explanation as though it was normal behaviour mid-journey in Yugoslavia. In my state, however, I was glad of the cessation of engine noise and car movement however brief.

Checking in at the hotel in Zagreb was done as fast as I could, the need for privacy and a lavatory being the most pressing issues. Clutching my room key plus a note someone had left at reception, I hastily accessed my room. By now my stomach was in full rebellion and I was at the mercy of uncontrollable diarrhoea. I was good for nothing but full-time nursing. Apart from a very daring excursion to a supermarket to purchase something to eat and drink that was plain enough for my stomach to not instantly reject, I remained confined to my room and debilitated for the whole of the three free days, dealing with what was obviously a bout of alcohol poisoning.

All of which was rather unfortunate. The note that had

accompanied my keys at reception was from the Yugoslavian pianist's stunning girlfriend from Radenci. It was simple, to the point and unanswered – My boyfriend is away for the week, give me a ring. Her Zagreb phone number was attached.

On our travels, the Quartet never quite made it as far as the Antipodes, getting no farther in an easterly direction than Hong Kong and Singapore in 1986. The few days in Hong Kong included a free day, which I passed criss-crossing Victoria harbour on a network of ferries. The network operated as a water bus service, providing a necessary means of transport for commuters, but it was also a wonderful way of lazily viewing the cityscape by drifting from one vantage point to another at little expense.

Many of the ferries had snack bars on board selling tasty indigenous street food – I'll avoid calling it junk food for obvious reasons – and an endless supply of tea, which made it a relatively calm and inexpensive way of escaping the hustle and bustle of dry land.

Andy, a close friend of Michael's from Edinburgh who lived in Hong Kong, invited us out for a meal one evening, together with his Chinese wife Tin and a friend of theirs called June. Andy was known to the rest of us, but only in passing when a rehearsal day in Michael's house might coincide with Andy calling in. He was now the project manager of an office tower block nearing completion in the city centre, Tin was an interior designer and June worked for the Hong Kong Police Department.

The food was authentic Chinese of course and the conversation was wide-ranging, settling at one point on the merits of eating an apple, complete with core and pips. June in particular was smitten at the idea of eating the whole fruit and had apparently never contemplated the possibility. We spent a preposterous amount of time elaborating on the topic, going off at comical tangents in all sorts of directions, which eventually brought the evening to a close.

The next morning, an apple-sized gift box arrived at my hotel room. Removing the ribbon, lifting the lid and unwrapping the cox's pippin was my second flattering encounter, which was also unreciprocated.

I'm sure that neither of these two brushes with suitors would qualify them as groupies as groupies are a rarity in the world of string quartets and when they do surface it's usually as maternal/fraternal figures, or just plain off-the-wall characters. Cathay Pacific was one of the sponsors for our Hong Kong Festival concerts and the wife of the managing director invited us to her house for tea one afternoon. Apart from the palatial property with its amazing views atop Victoria Peak, the only other thing I remember about the afternoon was the general conversation about other music groups that she had met over the years and when the name of the Lindsay Quartet came up, she had a fit of giggles. Once recovered, she explained that her giggling was prompted by memories of Ronnie Birks and his habit of making audible risqué asides, followed by a quick burst of hysterical laughter. She finished by saying, 'Ronnie was a very naughty boy.'

EIGHTEEN

Avoid synthetic materials and keep your dancing pumps close to hand. 'I'm not sure the Barynya is in our repertoire...'

I'm not sure how much, if at all, our tour of the Soviet Union in 1985 was influenced by our participation in the *Edinburgh Conversations* but, whatever the background, this tour was a most unusual event given the cultural vacuum that existed at the time. Also unusual was the negotiated method of payment. In the Soviet Union's desperation to open communications and reconnect with the West, it was agreed that only half our fee would be paid in the non-exchangeable local currency of roubles, with the other half paid in US dollars: for the entire fee not to be paid in the local currency was almost unheard of. The tour was made even more significant by being the last performances with Christopher, our cellist of the previous ten years.

Chris's role as cellist was coupled with that of administrator, for which he got paid a separate remuneration and over the last year or so, the rest of the Quartet had become disgruntled at his lack of success in this role. The EQ's diary of engagements had been dwindling year by year with little evidence that the Quartet's fortunes could be turned around by continuing with Chris's dogmatic approach.

This came to a head about three months before the Russian tour, when Mike, who Chris considered to be his greatest ally and myself arrive for a rehearsal on the day of a concert. As we walk into the empty church, the venue for that night's concert, we are complaining about Chris's fruitless administrative efforts. Mike in particular is giving out in very vituperative terms, a long and detailed critique, sparing little to the imagination. Shortly after finishing his tirade, from about three or four rows in front of where we are standing, Chris slowly rises from a pew, like a body from the grave in a 1960s Hammer Horror film. He has been lying down, resting not sleeping and of course has overheard every word.

A couple of days later Chris resigns, both as cellist and administrator, giving us a three-month period of notice.

It's March as we set off for Moscow and still very cold. Moscow for some unknown reason doesn't have the pleasure of an Edinburgh Quartet concert to look forward to, but we do spend our first night there, in one of the Soviet era's iconic Moscow hotels. It looks more like a poorly disguised military bunker, or perhaps an enormous concrete cake rather than an hotel.

We each have a suite of rooms, including entrance vestibule. Plenty of space but spartan in furnishing. A distinctive musty smell pervades my room. I guess responsibility for this not altogether objectionable odour, lies in the layers of ingrained dust, cigarette smoke and vodka accumulated over the years and meticulously polished into the many wooden surfaces: a singular aroma I have met before, indicative of a certain era of public buildings.

I spend some of my limited free time in Moscow visiting the Metropol Hotel, an Art Nouveau building with a magnificent stained glass ceiling high above its restaurant. I take a table in this spectacular room, order a drink and settle down with a book. The book is the autobiography of the infamous Russian spy, Kim Philby, which is deliberately chosen as Philby lives in Moscow and is known to frequent the Metropol. My hope is that the book will be made more vivid by soaking up the atmosphere of one of Philby's haunts and I might even catch a glimpse of the notorious double agent. I also hope that reading this book in public, if the subject matter is noticed, isn't seen as provocative.

No incident and no Philby, but the time has been well spent drinking in my surroundings and the very quaffable Russian champagne which is so cheap, you would be hard-pressed finding a cup of tea at the same price back home.

All our travel is done at night and almost exclusively by rail, presumably to stop us observing that which they would not like us to see. The sleeper cars are comfortable and comforting and each carriage comes with a large samovar, manned, or rather womanned by a regulation size uniformed female of no more than 4ft 8ins: the samovar takes up more space.

Our first concert is in Smolensk. We arrive mid-afternoon to find the hotel is not expecting us until the following day and we are going to have to wait a couple of hours before rooms can be made available. Our arrival also coincides with a wedding celebration in full swing and the hotel is buzzing. The whole of the ground floor is under siege including the foyer, our only source of refuge. We cower in what we think is an unobtrusive corner but are soon spotted and quickly pounced upon by a delegation of exuberant revellers and invited to join the party, an invitation so insistent a refusal is out of the question.

This is no society wedding. This is a marriage between two villagers whose families have chosen to celebrate in a big, city hotel. The band is raw and loud, the booze is flowing liberally and the dance floor is taking a hammering.

Partaking of vodka is our first enticement, followed by more vodka. Luckily, we don't have a concert this evening and, given the prevailing circumstances, are able to avoid the risk of offending anybody by gratefully accepting their hospitality. I can't remember the last time I slipped into my dancing pumps, a distant memory I'm more than certain I share with Chris and Michael. And Miles, I very much doubt has ever set foot on a dance floor, but there is no escaping it this time. After pointless protestations we are manhandled into the melee and tossed about like logs in a storm surge. These women are strong, but it's not the only show of strength in evidence. Predominantly dressed in nylon, or some other synthetic fibre, the overpowering odour of perspiration-soaked costumes is threatening to detract from this otherwise wonderfully unique and spontaneous experience.

We are being coveted by female after female and given star guest status. We are passed around and consumed as

Red Square, Moscow, 1985

rapidly as a plate of canapes that unexpectedly appears at a health farm. The fact that all four of us have only left feet doesn't seem to matter at all. Eventually, we are rescued by information from reception that our rooms are ready and although we are having a great time feel it's the right time to exit the proceedings, although not without a certain amount of determination.

The friendship, generosity and welcome we have received is life reaffirming and makes for another memorable touring moment.

After Smolensk, we next visit Tartu. We forsake the train for this journey and travel to this university city by minibus, making it the only journey we undertake by road. Our minibus driver is a woman in her thirties who makes a big impression when the minibus breaks down in the middle of nowhere and she sets about repairing it calmly and methodically. She retrieves a large toolbox from the boot, removes the cowling covering the gearbox which is located inside the cab and within half an hour we are on our way again. We are all impressed, but Miles as a non-driver is really astonished, as his closest understanding of the workings of a gearbox and its relationship to speed, would be a glossary of Italian terms indicating various music tempi.

On a visit to the State Hermitage Museum in Leningrad, I'm taken totally by surprise when I burst into tears while standing in front of a painting by Renoir. The whole gallery is rather run-down with extremely poor lighting and even a broken window here and there. There are few people and those that are here are swallowed up by the cavernous building. The tearful moment is definitely triggered by this portrait of a young woman, but I don't know why. I search myself for a connection between subject matter and my personal life but come up with nothing to which I can consciously attribute this emotional release.

To produce such a captivating work of art with perhaps a subliminal message hidden in the layers of pigment that maybe even Renoir was unaware of, has to be craftmanship at its greatest. I'm loath to leave the spot and continue staring at the painting for some considerable time, knowing that the emotion it has unleashed will evaporate once I detach myself and only the memory of this exquisite painting will remain.

Running is my fix and my prime method of distancing myself from the demands and stress of being a performing musician. I have a few marathons under my belt and last year in Edinburgh, I fulfilled my goal of running under three hours, by clocking up two hours, fifty-seven minutes. My running shoes, vest and shorts are always stashed away in my suitcase when I'm on tour. Leningrad is no exception. I have just bought some new gear back in Scotland, fully featuring Nike logos, not a familiar sight on the streets of Leningrad I imagine and have set off for a run around the city. I'm clutching a map, but in my usual fashion, still manage to get hopelessly lost. At one point I pass the main entrance of a military barracks bustling with activity. Armed sentries guard the open gates, with military vehicles and personnel constantly on the move. From my appearance in my somewhat loud running gear, it's obvious I'm a foreigner and just as obvious, as I stop to consult what is in my hand, that I'm clutching a map. I'm expecting some kind of reaction, however mild, but I'm ignored. It's as though I'm invisible. It crosses my mind that if the whole situation was reversed and transplanted to the USA, whether the reaction would be the same. . .

In Riga, on the shores of the Baltic Sea, we walk among huge icebergs washed up on the beach. In Tallinn, people wander about in sub-freezing temperatures eating ice-cream and among the imposing buildings enclosing the main square I spot several unusual lacquered front doors. The deep gloss of the doors reminds me of the lid on a grand piano, which is not surprising as this is the home of the world-famous 'Estonia' pianos.

Our last concert in Vilnius is the very last Edinburgh Quartet concert for Chris who I have known for fourteen years; before the EQ we shared the immediately preceding four years as colleagues in the Northern Sinfonia. At the time of my joining the Sinfonia, it was common knowledge that Chris enjoyed a drink or two, but shortly after I joined, he became teetotal and hasn't touched a drop of alcohol since (including the Smolensk wedding).

In anticipation of a sense of satisfaction and to enhance a feeling of relaxation morphing into celebration following this final concert, I had earlier procured a half bottle of vodka for consumption post-concert back at our barless hotel. Michael and Miles have also laid in some alcohol for our small celebration to mark the end of the tour.

After the concert and now in the empty lobby of our incredibly quiet hotel, we gather and settle down with our various bottles and a few nibbles. Chris is with us but taciturn. Relations have continued to be uncomfortable throughout his three-month period of notice and there's no chance the celebration we are now having is to mark his departure.

As I produce my half bottle of vodka, Chris leans across from his chair and with outstretched hand, asks brusquely if he can have a sip: this will be his first alcohol for nearly fourteen years. His request sounds more like a command and I pass the bottle. This is no time for the niceties of a glass and he fearlessly gulps down a healthy sized swig and the bottle stays firmly clutched in his hand. I'm so shocked by his relapse, I'm unable to find a way of asking for the return of my bottle. I'm consoled by kidding myself that as it's his final concert, I don't really object. This is fortunate as the bottle is without doubt staying securely where it is as another glug of vodka disappears with alarming speed. Chris has yet to speak but it soon becomes clear that his taciturnity is a prelude to a calculated diatribe edging ever closer. It's getting ever closer at about the same rate as my looked-forward-to vodka is disappearing. Within twenty minutes my vodka has all but vanished and Chris takes the floor. Like a judge giving his final summing-up, he delivers character assassinations on his soon-to-be ex-colleagues, He is completely uninhibited, mostly from the effect of the vodka – given the speed at which it has just been consumed, it's a miracle he can even speak – although there is another disinhibiting factor. Chris is a morose character who has always been pessimistic about dying at an early age. On more than one occasion he has dropped into general conversation that all male members of his family keel over at the age of fifty and so, in a spirit of family solidarity, he is expecting to depart imminently as he has recently attained this critical age. (He does in fact go on to lead an active life well into his eighties.)

With the half-bottle now consumed, Chris's resentment, which has been fermenting over the last three months, is now given full reign. I get off the lightest, as I've always been open in my criticism and nothing on my part in the overheard conversation back at the church three months earlier should have come as any surprise to him.

Miles comes in for a fair bit more flack than me. The problem with Miles is that he contributes nothing to the running of the Quartet other than playing his violin, not even a willingness to give up his personal time in order to discuss Quartet planning. The only exception is that once a year he does find a small amount of time to scribble down a basic repertoire list for the year ahead. Chris scolds him on this point and lists a number of his other shortcomings in some detail, mentioning his disappointment at Miles' overall lack of participation in the functioning of the Quartet.

Now it's Michael's turn to stand before the bench. Chris has been building up to this moment and his bitterness manifests itself in unbridled venom. Chris had always thought of Michael as the most supportive of the three of us and the overheard conversation must have come as a complete revelation. With much bitterness in his voice, he accuses him soundly of being two-faced and lets little else go unremarked upon.

Interestingly, criticism of all three of us is limited to our part in the running of the Quartet and no mention is made of musical issues. This may have been connected to one of our grouses three months earlier which concerned Chris's apparent lack of interest in musical matters which we suggested was having a deleterious effect on the quality of his playing. We had put this down to him spending too much time unproductively trying to procure large chunks of sponsorship money rather than methodically seeking basic work from the numerous music clubs.

Once Chris completes his summation, he simply rises from his chair, turns on his heels wishing us a curt good night and takes himself off to bed.

We are left sitting in a state of stunned silence at what we have just heard – and bemused by the tempering sight of Chris polishing off a half-bottle of vodka and calmly tottering off to his room. None of us seems unduly upset at what has just been said and if we are brutally honest with ourselves, the criticisms launched at each one of us should come as no real surprise. The air clears somewhat and the three of us continue our muted celebration with no shortage of material to chew over. In my vodka-less state, my thirst is quenched by the sharing of my colleagues' alcohol.

The next morning we meet at the hotel entrance ready for the journey to Moscow airport, that is all but our ex-cellist, leaving Elena, our Russian interpreter and minder to go and look for him. She soon returns with a forlorn Christopher who she had found still tucked up in bed, fast asleep.

He doesn't look too good but he is just about able and he shows no signs of remorse for what he said last night: why should he? There are signs of remorse detectable from his disconnected demeanour, but these are the consequence of his relapse and what it's now doing to his substantial frame.

An hour before we are due to depart, I lose my passport somewhere in Moscow airport. On reporting the loss I'm told that without it, I cannot depart and that I should enquire at the flight's departure gate. I'm more than a little concerned. I have visions of spending the rest of my life in a gulag trying to write poetry.

After an initial visit and several follow-up visits to the gate, my passport is providentially found a few minutes before the gate closes and handed to me with a grin. I have the distinct impression it has been at the gate all the time. Russian joke.

The Aeroflot flight is all but empty, a small but exclusive group of twelve. Joe Bugner the heavyweight boxer and Gerald Durrel the naturalist are two of those on board (Bugner was born in Szeged-Szoreg in Southern Hungary and by a twist of fate, this village is a few kilometres from where I now live). Bugner is enormous and unmissable, but it's Durrel who attracts attention. A very drunk and jolly middle-aged woman can't leave him alone. For much of the flight she stands in the aisle, leaning on the back of his seat and breathing alcohol fumes over him. She totters when excited and he is very lucky she doesn't flop into his lap during these moments of overzealous activity. Maybe his experience in dealing with undomesticated animals comes in handy, as he remains courteous throughout and tolerates her fawning behaviour with good humour. Who knows, he could be enjoying it.

The entertaining journey is a fitting finale to our Russian tour which has been full of entertainment, given and received and never to be forgotten.

The fate of the unexchangeable roubles is worth telling. I spent them naturally enough. Some for presents, Matryoshka dolls predictably at the top of the list and a beautiful black Palekh papier-mache lacquered box, hand painted in vibrant colours with gold leaf gilding, depicting in fine detail a Russian folk tale. I also bought for myself, a wind-up Paketa watch, a make and similar model to one worn by President Gorbachev, allegedly. It's adorning my wrist at this very moment, thirty-five years later. My final purchase was a violin.

By 1985, I have a son called Dominic, six years old and this violin is for him. It would be better described as a toy instrument rather than a proper violin, although it is playable. It has four strings tuned to the correct pitch and a bow of sorts, that after much applying of heavy-duty rosin can draw something approximating a musical sound. It's a violin that B&Q would be proud to have on their shelves. Dominic receives this present with a surprising amount of enthusiasm and immediately gives it a go. He has never tried playing before and for some strange reason, is surprised that he is unable to instantly thrash out *Twinkle, twinkle. . .* I make some encouraging noises and by bedtime he is damaged so little by this setback, he happily toddles off to bed clutching his Russian Strad in its soft case.

Morning departure from Moscow, 1985

Replacing the crowing of cockerels at dawn next morning, the dulcet tones of Dominic playing his violin waft through to my bedroom as he attempts another rendition of a musical masterpiece. I go through to his room to find him sitting up in bed cradling his violin, complaining that he still can't play.

It was possibly cruel of me, but Dom had slept through the night with the Strad under his pillow. I had jokingly suggested the night before that, as in the folktale about sleeping with a book under your pillow and the contents of the book being magically implanted into the sleeper's memory, the same logic might be applied to learning the violin.

I'm happy to report that, like my watch, Dominic is also still ticking over on the violin thirty-five-years later – needless to say, not on the Russian Strad, although I do still have it.

NINETEEN

A swan's composure can only be fully understood if one peers below the surface.

Chris's legacy in his administrative and fund-raising role wasn't all bad. It was only towards the end of his ten years in the Edinburgh Quartet that things really soured. During that time, the way the Arts were funded was also undergoing a sea change.

In the 1960s and 70s, Arts organisations relied almost entirely upon public bodies for their funding: the Arts Council, the British Council and local authorities. Total business sponsorship for the Arts in 1975 in the UK amounted to a mere £500,000, but that was all about to change. The American model of commercial sponsorship was being ushered in, changing the complexion of arts organisations for ever. Support from public bodies was still a necessary component of funding, but sponsorship from the private sector became essential as the hard-pushed public sector could no longer take on full responsibility with costs ever rising. The pair were further strengthened and a few years later when the National Lottery Fund joined in to produce a three-pronged alliance.

With this change of focus, came a great deal more accountability. Arts organisations now collaborate closely with sponsors who can have a substantial influence on how their donated money should be used, especially in terms of advertising and image. Sponsorship itself has become a marketing tool for the sponsor's business. Lottery funding on the other hand is dependent on successful applications for the financing of specific projects.

These complex methods of funding orchestras have necessitated vastly enlarged administrations, in some cases almost to the size of that being administered. In the 1980s, on operating a similar workload to that of today, the Scottish Chamber Orchestra, numbering thirty-seven was run by a manager, an assistant manager and a van driver. The job of librarian, fixer (someone who engages extra players) and stage manager was done by Barry Collarbone, the 2nd trumpet. This efficient small band of four has since been replaced by an administration of thirty-four!

An irony not to be missed is that most of the office staff work a permanent salaried contract, whereas in many orchestras, the SCO being one, players are paid only for hours worked.

Over time Chris' efforts for securing finances became confined to only two areas of the Quartet, that of gaining commercial sponsorship on the one hand and residencies with educational institutions on the other. Both were failing miserably. The thinking behind his approach was that, if successful, it would produce guaranteed regular income over several years, producing a degree of financial security that searching anew every year could not do, making the work-reward ratio more than justified. His obsession was in fact based on a previous highly lucrative partnership.

At the height of his powers and through a connection provided by Miles, Chris had pulled off a real coup in the form of a hefty sponsorship deal with Standard Life Assurance Company. Miles was a good friend of an amateur flautist who just happened to be the general manager of Standard Life. A couple of months after Miles had initiated the connection, Chris finalised the deal and a day was chosen to announce the generous support to the world. He was not slow to realise the full value of exploiting this announcement and organised a day of publicity in several strands to gain maximum effect.

The itinerary for the day read: meet at the Standard Life Building at the end of George Street in the morning, then parade through the streets of Edinburgh in a vintage open-top car, followed by a press conference and short performance by the Quartet back at George Street. Finally, through to Glasgow and the studios of Scottish Television for an afternoon rehearsal, as we had been allotted a lengthy ten-minute item on the 6.30pm Scottish national evening news. This STV slot was courtesy of another good friend of Miles who was the music director at STV, Arthur Blake.

As is apparent, Miles's contribution through his personal connections had played a significant part in getting to this point, but unfortunately as it turns out, not all Miles' friends had the same sense of loyalty and the day is destined to be far removed from the day of celebration we had imagined.

We all gather – well, almost all – at the designated hour

Promotional photo, Hopetoun House, South Queensferry, 1988

in George Street where the vintage car emblazoned with suitable publicity waits at kerbside. Three musicians clutching instrument cases are ready to enter the stage, but where is Miles? He is normally a good timekeeper. We can do no more than just wait, as Miles can't be contacted because he stubbornly refuses to own a mobile phone.

Five minutes turns into fifteen, still no Miles. We presume he has either got his times muddled up, or more likely, sitting uncomfortably in a taxi or bus held up by the congested traffic of central Edinburgh. As there's a precise schedule to follow, we decide to set off in the vintage car with Bert standing in as honorary 1st violin, in the hope that Miles will have arrived on our return to George Street.

Bert is delighted at this instant ennoblement and throws himself into his new role with alacrity, performing to a higher standard than a reserved Miles could possibly have done. His energetic waving and gesturing as we roam the thoroughfares of Edinburgh draws attention in bucket-loads from the bemused population.

When we return to George Street, there is still no sign of Miles, which immediately creates a serious problem. Without Miles, there can be no performance (there's a limit to Bert's talents) and the press conference will now have to be a pared down affair, with severely restricted photo shoot.

At the time there were two violinists of pre-eminence in Scotland, one was Miles Baster and the other, Leonard Friedman, founder/director of the Scottish Baroque Ensemble. The personalities of the two couldn't have been more different, even though their circumstances had much in common. They were of a similar age, lived alone, with both heavily reliant on Edinburgh taxis as neither could drive. One trait that they did share was what appeared to be a *fear of success/fear of failure*. When work was flourishing, they both had the ability to sabotage it just at the point when the next step-up professionally looked attainable. It's as though they were comfortable, confident and able at a certain level and feared that moving away from that spot would cause the whole pack of cards to collapse.

At the end of the truncated press conference in Edinburgh, optimism was beginning to run low; the hope of Miles suddenly turning up was looking increasingly unlikely. What was looking more likely was that the significant evening news slot on STV, without the Quartet's captain, will just slip silently beneath the airwaves. Chris's wife Sheena, who played a large part in helping Chris in his managerial role, was now enlisted to track down Miles by visiting his flat, a rented Council flat on the tenth floor of a block in the Gilmerton district of Edinburgh, not renowned for the number of violinists living therein.

Meantime we made our way to Glasgow kidding ourselves that Miles had somehow totally confused the timing of the day's events and will be there waiting for us. Miles was not at STV, nor was he in his flat. Sheena had made every effort to find him, at and around his flat, making enquiries of neighbours, without any luck. There was nothing more we could do but sit the afternoon out as the big day disappeared unheeded like the Arctic ice cap.

Our schedule now became secondary to that of a national television company's and the time came when STV's generous slot dissipated into nothing more than a mention in a list of minor news stories of the day. Fortunately, the sponsorship was secure, but we had lost out on a huge publicity opportunity. Grave concern for Miles' whereabouts was now uppermost on our minds as we headed despondently for Queen's Street station and the journey back to Edinburgh.

The next day was a scheduled rehearsal day which had been arranged earlier in the week. At ten-o-clock, only a trio was in attendance; worryingly, still no sign of Miles. We wrote off the rehearsal amid these rising concerns and Sheena volunteered to make a second visit to his flat. Still no sign of him.

A full twenty-four hours passes before Sheena makes a

third attempt. This time the door was eventually opened by a very distraught Miles. He looked terrible. Some of his fingernails were torn and he is bowed with remorse and very tearful.

Miles was normally fiercely self-reliant, but Sheena instantly saw that in his present fragile state, he was in no condition to refuse her help. She persuaded this broken man to forgo his independence for once and come and spend a few days with her and Chris and their three daughters in the hope that time spent in the bosom of a normal functioning family will lift his depression and get him back on his feet.

The initial worry concerning Miles' disappearance was now over and the mystery surrounding his lost forty-eight hours slowly emerges over the next few days.

Brought up as a strict Catholic, sent to a boarding preparatory school at the age of four and only at home with his parents for the school holidays can't have been an easy start in life for Miles. During World War Two, he was evacuated to live with a family in Cornwall, followed by boarding at King's School, Canterbury and then on to Oxford University to study Classics, a course he dropped out of in his first year to pursue a career in music. Having started to learn the violin at the age of six and showing a prodigious talent right from the start, he soon came to realise during that Oxford year that the only thing he really wanted to do, was play his violin.

He was Leader of the National Youth Orchestra of Great Britain in his teens and after leaving Oxford, went on to study at the Royal Academy of Music in London for four years, followed by a year at the Julliard School of Music in New

York and almost immediately upon arriving back from the USA, he was approached by Edinburgh University.

He was considered Britain's most promising violinist at the time, so in 1959, armed with this knowledge, Sydney Newman, the Dean of the Music Faculty at Edinburgh University, recruited Miles with a brief to form a resident string quartet within the year.

Meanwhile, Miles was dealing with the fact that he was gay, but not openly so, as it was socially unacceptable at the time, not to mention illegal (until 1980). Other demons yapping at his heels in the years to come would be the disappearance of the father he hardly knew on his way to work, a gambling addiction which after heavy losses he managed to conquer, a forty-a-day smoking habit and an unconquered preponderance for binge drinking. A brilliant but flawed character it would be fair to say.

Miles revealed that on the evening before the Standard Life day, he went on a bender with some of his friends, friends of questionable pedigree. He remembered little of the ensuing hours, but in putting things together with the help of a few witnesses, a couple of victims and the police, it appeared that late into the evening, this band of reprobates took to the streets, carousing with the help of a mix of stimulants, until one of their number slammed a house brick through a random bungalow's large front window, after which they all scarpered, except Miles.

I'm sure that Miles, however drunk, would have realised the gravity of what had just happened and will have made no attempt to flee. And when confronted by the deeply distressed elderly homeowners, was rooted to the spot until the police arrived and took him into custody. He spent the night in a cell in the local police station before being released the next day, making his way back to his tenth-floor council flat in Gilmerton and barricading himself behind his locked door for the best part of two days, until Sheena finally made contact.

Miles made good progress with the sympathetic support of Chris and family and was able to return home within three or four days. The Quartet's usual routine soon returned to normal, with Miles displaying amazing resilience to what must have been a very traumatic experience.

As well as valuing his independence, Miles was a very private individual, not one to share his emotions or divulge details of his personal life and so any practical repercussions of the incident stay concealed and the episode was never revisited.

TWENTY

When performing, a variety of positions can be considered. 'Would a pillow help?'

Supplementing my earnings from the Edinburgh Quartet by deputising with other ensembles not only helped to give me a respectable income, it also brought variety. Diversity in the form of a completely different repertoire was one benefit and working with other musicians was always refreshing, providing valuable new musical experiences and ideas that I could take back to the Quartet. Being involved in an outstanding performance awakens all sorts of thoughts and emotions that one can learn from. A simple rule of thumb from the conductor Rudolf Schwarz for the performance of symphonies from the Classical era that always worked well, especially those of Schubert: perform fast movements slowly and slow movements quickly. And personal insights from soloists and conductors provided stimulation concerning all facets of interpretation including mood, phrasing and particular composers' musical intentions: anger and roughness in

Beethoven, passion in Mozart, humour in Haydn, rebellion in Shostakovitch. Visiting soloists and conductors from a myriad of backgrounds also kept everything up to date, having perhaps been in New York, Sydney, or Shanghai the week before.

The Scottish Chamber Orchestra was the ensemble with which I most frequently deputised. An orchestra of a remarkably high standard, with an eclectic range of programmes, performed in a wide-ranging mix of venues. One of the more notable concert days was a series of performances in unusual settings which were accessed throughout the day by rail.

The train, comprised of 1950s railway carriages pulled by a nostalgia-inducing steam locomotive with its unmistakeable redolence, puffed its way through the Highlands from Inverness to the terminus at the Kyle of Lochalsh, a stone's throw from the Isle of Skye. The train would stop occasionally to allow the mobile audience and their picnic hampers to disembark and listen to a concert on Plockton beach, an hotel terrace at the Kyle of Lochalsh, or some other equally curious setting. Entertainment was also provided when in motion by perhaps a violin and viola duo, a cello sonata (an upright piano was always deployed in the mailcoach for the day), or any instrumental combination that was small enough to be accommodated.

Like most orchestras, the SCO was full of interesting characters. One such character was the Principal 2nd violin, Peter Bramble Jelly (not his real name, but pretty close) and more often than not, I partnered Peter on the front desk.

Peter was somewhat of a chameleon. On the surface, an affable, easy-going personality, keeping to himself most of the time, but deep down a different persona rumbled. He could be quite extreme in his likes and dislikes of people and instead of showing his feelings in a confrontational manner, chose to amuse himself by taking a humorous path. His awareness of the possibility of humour in most situations was never far away and he had that enviable ability to create a highly comical scene, leaving onlookers fighting back outbursts of giggling while he calmly maintained a cool exterior.

The composer, Peter Maxwell Davies (later to become Master of the Queen's Musick and a resident of the island of Hoy, one of the Orkney islands) was an obvious irritant for him, especially when Maxwell Davies was conducting one of his own compositions. And when, from 1986 to 1996, Max, as he was affectionately known, wrote a massive body of work for the SCO under the title of the 'Strathclyde Concertos' (ten altogether, with soloists from within the orchestra and recorded by the SCO), then Peter B.J. was in his element.

I can't remember Max ever displaying a sense of humour. His rapport with the orchestra might well have benefitted from introducing a few lighter moments during rehearsals. Paul McCreesh suggesting the sound of a passage should reflect the bouncy manner of Rupert Bear's walk and Frans Brüggen comparing awkward lumpy playing to a toilet roll fitted to its holder in such a way that the paper unfolds away instead of towards you, are two memorable and endearing examples.

When it came to recording these concertos, the process most often applied and the one employed in this case, was that of recording large chunks of music, then, while the soloist and conductor joined the producer and sound engineer in the sound box to listen to what had been recorded, the orchestra is left sitting in their seats, with nothing to do but wait. A number of small retakes might follow, with the same procedure being repeated throughout the day, making recording sessions a contrasting mixture of tension and boredom.

Rather than just twiddling his thumbs, Peter B.J. liked to occupy himself during these silent periods of inactivity by playing Boggle, harmless enough unless put in the hands of someone bent on revenge. . .

Anyone familiar with Boggle, knows that each game only lasts three minutes and between each game, the plastic container holding the six heavy dice-size cubes on which the letters are displayed is shaken to rearrange the letters. In the hands of PBJ this becomes a weapon and I guarantee that the amount of noise a shaken Boggle container can make would not go unnoticed in a large percussion section in full spate.

Unlike most conductors, Max didn't go to the sound box to listen, but stayed sitting at the podium for most of the playbacks, preferring to study his score and rely on the producer's advice over the intercom. What better conditions for a game of Boggle? Peter calculatingly picked his moments and delighted in lengthy and vigorous Boggle- shaking, frantic enough to suggest his life depended on it, right under Max's nose.

For Peter, *this* was the game, not Boggle and Max took the bait every time, showing his annoyance in equal measure to the amount of satisfaction Peter gained from his successful ploy. It became a constant throughout the day as Peter is scolded and asked repeatedly, 'Just do it more quietly,' or, 'Do you really have to do that?'

Peter employed a range of replies which were always delivered in pathetic tones, like, 'Oh, I'm terribly sorry Max, I'll try to do it more quietly.' or, 'I'm so sorry Max, I forgot. I'll try and remember next time.'

I wonder if Peter was familiar with one of my favourite little pieces, Farewell to Stromness. If so, one might have thought this short simple and evocative melody for piano written by Max might have softened his irritation. The only other piece by Max, Orkney Wedding with Sunrise, which I can happily hear anytime for its accessibility and effectiveness was very familiar to Peter, but this didn't appear to interfere with his enthusiasm for Boggle either.

Peter didn't necessarily need an excuse to be mischievous, sometimes he simply delighted in the exercise. This was familiar behaviour and could be unnerving for those seated close to him. The orchestra's Leader, Jim Clark, was a man of sizeable proportions and when he crossed his legs, as he often did during rehearsals, his trouser legs tended to ride up above his considerable calves, exposing a large expanse of white skin. Peter sometimes felt compelled to react to this inelegance and would mimic Jim by crossing his own legs, but with his trouser legs exaggeratingly pulled up to his knees. He would hold this position within Jim's eyeline for a good five minutes at a time, but I was never ever aware that Jim picked up on this. An orchestra is akin to being back at school in more ways than one.

It must be quite apparent by now, that orchestras can be a great source of humour and those members with an acute sense of humour, can use the whole orchestra like an instrument to be played upon. A character with an ability to do this, time and time again was the cellist Kevin McCrae of the Scottish Chamber Orchestra, the same Kevin McCrae who auditioned for the Edinburgh Quartet in 1985. Kevin died much too young at the age of forty-four, but accounts of his profligate antics still circulate.

Kevin was a remarkable musician, well known for his great versatility as a pianist and composer/arranger, as well as cellist and his prowess for creating humour was on a par with these musical skills. Sometimes, when combining these two gifts, the result could be priceless. One of his pranks I remember well took place in the Usher Hall during a rehearsal for a Mozart piano concerto.

Sir Charles Mackerras was conducting the opening tutti, playing it through before the pianist arrived, with the grand piano already in place, centre stage. After we finished playing the opening tutti and before Mackerras could begin rehearsing, the expected silence was broken as the piano miraculously came to life, perfectly producing the solo piano part. Unbeknown to Mackerras and most of the orchestra, Kevin had put down his cello a few bars before the end of the tutti and shielded by a forest of music stands, chairs and instruments, had surreptitiously crawled under the piano.

From there, he turned on to his back with his head directly under the keyboard, extended his arms upwards and in a position more suitable for replacing the exhaust on a car, played the opening piano statement faultlessly.

Mackerras, who had his back to the piano was completely unaware that Kevin was about to make his Usher Hall piano debut and like the rest of the orchestra, collapsed with laughter. The effect of Kevin's piano debut at the Usher Hall was hilarious, tinged with admiration at Kevin's execution of such a caper.

Incidentally, Kevin and Peter had earlier formed a piano trio, which must have been united among other things, by their corresponding sense of humour.

Kevin's closest friend was another SCO cellist called Neil Johnstone. They were inseparable during their time together in the orchestra, with a friendship going back to their school days when they were both members of the National Youth Orchestra of Scotland. Their escapades are legendary, many associated with the consumption of alcohol.

On one of the SCO's tours to Spain, a flight was needed to get from one end of Spain to the other in time for a concert that same evening. Everyone had checked in, including the cello section. The male half of the section then set about medicating itself against the fear of flying, in the time-honoured way. When the flight was first called, Kevin and Neil appeared to miss the announcement. They then missed the next call and all subsequent calls and finally the flight itself. Their serious dedication to achieving exactly the right quantity of medication proved to be too great a distraction.

But it was imperative that they should arrive for that evening's concert: half the cello section missing wasn't acceptable. There were no other flights available and no alternative rail or bus links, leaving them with only one avenue to explore – the hiring of a taxi.

After many hours and several hundred pounds lighter, they did arrive in time. The bill was paid by the management and later deducted from their salaries, wiping out all their earnings for the entire tour.

A less humorous set of occurrences are linked to Spain when our family embarked on a week-long holiday in the Basque region in the early 1980s. My partner Niamh, a violinist with the Scottish Chamber Orchestra, had just finished a Spanish tour with the orchestra, playing her final concert in San Sebastian. Before the tour, we had arranged for me and the children to join her there and once there, go in search of a suitable base for a seaside holiday on the rugged Atlantic coast.

In the morning after the final concert and a night's stay in San Sebastian, we headed westwards along the coast. With children and luggage in tow and after a short train journey, we trudged the streets of a small seaside town called Zarautz in search of accommodation. After the removal of a fair bit of shoe leather, we managed to rent a small apartment with spectacular views over Zarautz bay.

It was a perfect holiday spot for the children; sandcastle-sandy beach, shallow water and temperatures kept comfortably cool by the Atlantic Ocean. Dom's day was made, when this seven-year-old's eyes lit on a bar called Bum.

In the centre of the town, we discovered a charming traditional plaza, now pedestrianised, where we spent a good deal of time when not at the beach, supping local wine while the children ran around safely. There was a bandstand at one end which worked wonders as a climbing frame for the children and the original merchant's houses that enclosed the plaza had been converted into a plethora of bars and shops.

We attached ourselves to one bar in particular as it was intriguingly different from all the others. The walls were covered by a montage of photos of Basque political figures and judging by its clientele, it was unmistakably a meeting place for those sympathetic to Herri Batasuna, the politically extreme wing of the Basque Separatist Movement. This organisation was actively involved in bombings and shootings all over Spain and was more than capable of mounting sporadic terrorist attacks even on foreign soil. A few years earlier, in 1980, four police officers had been murdered by members of Herri Batasuna right there in Zarautz.

Being encumbered by two young children and a bedtime to consider, late afternoon and early evening were the times when we frequented the bar, always sitting outside on the terrace so we could keep an eye on the pair of them. It was never busy at that time and more often than not, we found ourselves in the company of the same woman aged about forty, who usually sat alone. It was not long before this circumstance encouraged us to make conversation. Her English was good and besides making small talk, we quizzed her on local matters: events, restaurants, things to see and do. She was cool but helpful and we had intermittent conversations throughout the week over a glass of rioja or jug of sangria. The week soon passed with a routine that varied little and we made our way back to Edinburgh.

Several months later, I was back in Spain with the Quartet, but this time at the opposite end of the country. We arrived at Malaga airport in the early hours of the morning and hired a taxi for the sixty-two-kilometre journey to Marbella, a journey we were lucky to survive. It was the most unnerving drive I've ever been subjected to, even more frightening than the taxi ride to the top of Corcovado in Rio de Janeiro.

The taxi was a battered old Seat saloon, only just big enough inside for the four of us plus small instruments, so the cello and four suitcases had to be stowed on the roof. This was not a problem for our over-relaxed driver as he set about unceremoniously and haphazardly fastening the precious cargo to the roof rack. Our obvious consternation at his careless lashings was brushed aside effusively, ensuring a sky-high level of anxiety before the journey had even begun. The final nail in the coffin came as we set off and realised once the doors were closed, that the alcohol fumes filling the car's interior were emanating from our driver. Our fear concerning his ability to drive safely were compounded by recognising that with cigarette in mouth, he also represented a serious fire hazard!

He tackled the road to Marbella like a skier, appearing to

use roadside objects as gates on a slalom course as he abruptly slewed from one directional correction to the next, in an attempt to keep the top-heavy car upright (I'd swear we were periodically attached to the tarmac by only two wheels). No amount of protestation made a blind bit of difference and only by providence did we arrive in one piece.

After checking in at the hotel, it was still early morning, but not quite early enough to make it worthwhile grabbing a few hours' sleep. There was some British political news that I was eager to find out about and thought that as Marbella was full of expats, there would be a newsagent open at daybreak, selling international newspapers. After five minutes of walking on completely deserted streets, a couple of figures appeared, approaching from the opposite direction. As they got closer and their features became distinct, I recognised one of the two women. Astonishingly, she was the woman from the bar in Zarautz.

'Hello, how are you?' I said as we were about to pass each other.

'Hello,' she replied, looking confused and uncomprehending.

'Don't you remember me from the bar in Zarautz?'

'Yes,' was her simple response and it was clear she didn't want to engage in conversation. We had a short, polite exchange but her parting words were unusual and seemed somehow weighted with omniscience. 'Go safely and in peace,' she said.

My search for a paper proved to be fruitless and I returned to the hotel to ruminate on what had just taken place. It was an extraordinary coincidence and as I thought more about it, a theory formed which begun to make the coincidence seem a little less exceptional.

Could this woman have been an active member of the Basque Separatist movement? Quite possibly from what I had observed in Zarautz. Herri Batasuna was known to be targeting areas with a high density of tourists, a category which Marbella fitted into for sure. Was she reconnoitring as part of a bombing campaign, or had she just planted a bomb? My imagination was now in full flight.

Another theory occurred to me, this one from her perspective: was this supposed Englishman not really an innocent foreigner, but someone recruited by the Spanish secret police department, disguised as a tourist, with a brief to observe the movements and personnel at the bar in Zarautz and was now following up his findings in Marbella? But serendipity had come into play and by a stroke of bad luck on his part, he had revealed himself by this accidental early morning encounter.

Nothing untoward befell the town of Marbella around this time so I have no way of confirming whether either of my two theories were correct, however frustrating that might be. And I don't even like spy thrillers.

TWENTY-ONE

It's not necessary to invest a fortune in purchasing your chosen instrument – especially if you are going to be crossing borders!

Beirut was synonymous with conflict rather than anything else in the latter years of the twentieth century, from the Lebanese civil war and interdenominational feuding, to being under siege from Syria in 1978 and again under siege by Israel in 1982. It sits at the centre of the Middle East's most volatile region, having borders with both Syria and Israel and is in constant dispute over demarcation of the Gaza Strip. The area is seldom totally tranquil.

In 1996 we had a trip to Beirut, shortly after the civil war had ended. Our first concert was the most important and took place in a bombed-out church that had been partially restored. It was in the presence of the Prime Minister, Rafiq Hariri and was also being broadcast live on national television. So far, so good.

The concert takes place on the third day of our visit, which is fortunate, because my luggage, containing my music isn't on the carousel when we arrive at Beirut airport. I'm the only member of the Quartet to suffer this minor inconvenience, but I'm confident I can manage without a toothbrush until the following day when the next flight from the United Kingdom arrives. I do get a bit of stick from the others, who always keep the music to be played at the first performance of a tour in their instrument case, to avoid this precise eventuality (instruments don't go in the hold).

Disaster. My suitcase is not on the next flight – and won't be on the following one either. The airline informs me that they have located it, which is good news, but that it's on its way to the USA is not such good news. Even worse, it won't be in Beirut in time for the performance: time to buy a toothbrush. Also, time to find replacement music. I quickly discover that obtaining the missing music here in Lebanon will be impossible, leaving only one course of action open.

Back in Edinburgh, Ken, a retired bank manager and voluntary helper operating the Quartet's office while we are away, is contacted and instructed to head straight for Edinburgh Central Library to source the required music and fax it out to Beirut. Ken is reliable and diligent and gets to work instantly. Over the next few hours, the main problem of my lost luggage is overcome when reems of 2nd violin music arrive via fax. This only leaves the issue of my missing concert clothes.

The Lebanese music agent who has booked us, appropriately named Mozart, comes to the rescue. He has a son who has a Versace franchise in Beirut and Mr Mozart junior invites me to his shop to rummage through his discontinued stock for something suitable. I find everything I need. Not a proper dinner jacket, but a perfectly acceptable replacement in dark blue, matched with a pair of black trousers which will more than suffice. Mr Mozart junior is exceedingly generous and as a bonus, he only charges me a nominal sum for clothes normally well out of my budget.

All set then? Not quite. The worst is yet to come as the concert gets underway. . .

The body of this incomplete church is equipped with lighting to highlight the restoration work, a lighting system which is quite the opposite of what is needed to read music. It is set pointing upwards rather than downwards. To help, an improvised lighting system has been provided which is barely adequate and is almost cancelled out by yet another battery of lights illuminating us from the front for the television coverage.

There's something else. If you are familiar with fax paper you will realise what my major hurdle of the evening is going to be. For those not familiar, I will elaborate. Fax paper is extremely flimsy and as it originates from a roll of paper, it continues curling in on itself once printed – and whatever you do to uncurl it, it fights back. So, I have to control dozens of separate sheets of curling Izal-toilet-paper-quality pages of undersize and faintly printed music. And the whole time I'm playing, I have to try to stop the pages curling up like petal heads closing down for the night. Coincidentally Izal is the name of a village in northern Lebanon. Somehow, I get away with it by awkwardly leaning more towards my music stand

and using the scroll end of my violin as a restraint and as each page passes, I consign it to an ever-growing pile of discarded pages at my feet. All pages were present and in correct order with none falling to the floor during the performance and after the most uncomfortable ninety minutes of concentrated terror I have ever experienced on the platform, sheer relief is the only emotion I'm capable of.

Incidentally, Rafiq Hariri was assassinated by a car bomb in 2005.

From Lebanon, we went overland to Syria and while passing through a wooden shack of a checkpoint at the border in the middle of nowhere, we bump into John Simpson, the BBC's World Affairs Editor, the only other traveller there. Though he appeared world-weary and preoccupied by the border guard's belligerent behaviour, he was happy to exchange a few words with us. The machine-gun-toting border guard's procrastination is bringing out his truculent side, which must be close to the surface most of the time, after years of similar encounters.

When it's time for our interrogation, we are asked to write down the value of our instruments and belatedly, just before handing over the figures, one of us thinks it pertinent to enquire why. The answer is simple and requires an immediate revaluation of our figures. The original piece of paper is hastily destroyed and a replacement completed and handed over with new and totally fictitious amounts of something like £20, £30, £15 and £10. The armed militia-type guards need the valuations, as they say we are obliged to pay 20% tax on the value of the instruments. They have no idea of the true value and seem quite content with our low estimates, as no doubt the so-called tax (probably as fabricated as our instrument valuations) is going straight into their pockets. We are happy to cough up having just saved a small fortune we don't have.

A visit to a Turkish bath was something I had never done and Damascus seemed like a good place for a baptism. The luxury hotel we were staying at offered the usual variety of modern ablutions, but that was not what I was looking for. I wanted a more authentic experience which I was told could be found in the old quarter of central Damascus.

I found what I was searching for easily enough and checked in. After parting with the tiny admission fee, I set off, not knowing what to expect, armed only with a towel and rudimentary instructions. It was something akin to a pedestrianised version of a ghost train at a fairground. As I advanced through a series of stone clad rooms half seen through the all-pervading steam, I'm battered by strong jets of water, pummelled by hands belonging to burly assistants who loom out of the steam and a couple of times in this subterranean world, I'm just left to sweat. Thirty minutes later sees the torture complete and the ghostly apparitions left behind and I emerge from the ordeal to be given a fresh towel, a mug of liquid sugar masquerading as tea and advised to take a seat on an Arabic style bench, which was so high off the ground, that with a mugful of tea in one hand, I found impossible to mount without the aid of an attendant. I was the only customer and enjoyed this moment of solitary repose, as the previous thirty minutes had been far from relaxing. It had been well worthwhile and I felt rejuvenated, with my head full of positive thoughts and ready to face the unpleasant walk back to the hotel along a road teeming with noisy polluting traffic.

On our way to Cairo, we passed through Jordan, with a brief stop in Amman where we gave a concert at a specialist music school. The staff and pupils were so welcoming at what for them was a rarity and I had a sense of embarrassment, realising the difficult conditions under which they coped. The building was in a poor state of repair and very basically equipped, but in spite of this, their spirit was indomitable. Enthusiastically, they quizzed us with an endless number of queries, wanting to know all about us, our instruments and the music we played. The short but rewarding visit was another reminder of the privileged life I have led.

While checking in at the Marriot Hotel in Cairo, music could be heard coming from another part of the hotel. It was obviously live music not muzak and although we couldn't see the performers, we recognised the sound as coming from a small mixed ensemble of wind and string instruments. Our curiosity gets the better of us and we dumped our luggage near the front desk before even checking in and followed the stream of music to its source in the dining room. The ensemble comprises five young Egyptian musicians – and we knew three of them.

Every August for twenty years, the Edinburgh Quartet had been engaged as resident ensemble, both as performers and tutors at the Aberdeen International Youth Festival. A vast number of events took place over the twelve-day festival, which was primarily a performing platform for orchestras and choirs. In tandem with this, a chamber music course operated at which we were the string tutors. Three years previous to this Cairo visit, a group of Egyptian music students had attended this course, of which three were now sitting in front of us.

We waited for them to finish their set, surprised them by our presence and enjoyed a warm reunion.

The Middle East was a regular haunt for the Quartet since an original visit in the 1980s as a result of some inspired lateral thinking on Mike's behalf. We had recently promoted a series of concerts in Hopetoun House, a stately home just outside Edinburgh and hundreds of unused flyers advertising the series were now left over. Frustratingly, these would normally be confined to the rubbish bin and considered an acceptable loss. On this occasion, Mike came up with the clever ruse that although the concert information on the flyers was out of date, exposure of our name and contact details on these classy-looking flyers might still have some value.

Mike put his lateral thinking immediately to the test and with a quick visit to Edinburgh airport, liberally sprinkled EQ flyers on every flat surface he could find, hastily disposing of the lot before drawing unwanted attention from the airport authorities. Unlike today and the emergence of the internet, the eighties relied almost entirely on printed matter for advertising and posters and flyers were everywhere, although not usually displayed in such a feral way as Mike's deployment.

Within two days, we had a phone call from the wife of the man in charge of the whole British Petroleum operation in Saudi Arabia, asking if we would be available for a short tour of the Middle East and if so, could we let her know how much we charged.

Two weeks later a tour of seven evening and three children's concerts had been organised. From there, things escalated and every year from that point, we regularly visited most of the countries of the Middle East. We played almost exclusively to expats, mainly in embassies, hotels, or company compounds, with the differing political and religious limitations of each country dictating the choice of venue. Due to these restricting circumstances and the concentration of expats, the paucity of Western entertainment in most of the oil-rich Arab countries meant our presence was warmly appreciated and came with a captive audience. In Saudi Arabia, the strict religious laws forbade gatherings with mixed audiences and the ploy of giving concerts within company compounds was a way of getting round that. This was still no guarantee of complete security and a raid by the authorities was always a possibility, ensuring that a great deal of nervousness hung in the air for many concerts. In Riyadh, the use of embassies as venues provided a more protective shield and was a successful way of avoiding disruption.

One of our trips came on the heels of the first Gulf War in 1991. We gave three concerts at the British Embassy in Riyadh, staying at the ambassador's residency for those three days. I was astonished to hear the ambassador, in a casual conversation with us, offer the information that one-hundred-thousand body bags had been ordered by the British forces in anticipation of enormous losses. I found this an outrageous possible outcome to contemplate, but even more shocking, was that this expectation was deemed acceptable. For me it was stark evidence of how many lives the British Government was prepared to callously lose in this region of the world in order to protect a supply of oil, a strategically important military presence and numerous business interests including the arms trade.

Another of the ambassador's snippets of information was slightly less dark and involved delivery of the embassy's new grand piano. On the day of its arrival at Dammam docks, the ambassador received an urgent phone call informing him that the piano was leaking. A leaking piano wouldn't normally be seen as a likely cause of a diplomatic incident, but worryingly this piano was leaking whisky. The large crate containing the piano had been seen as a perfect opportunity to smuggle in a good quantity of Scotch whisky into a country where alcohol is forbidden. The British Embassy wasn't the only embassy to circumvent the law on alcohol; they were all at it.

During a visit another year, we performed in the Mexican Embassy, a grand edifice with majestic entrance hall, with a double staircase arranged in a horseshoe shape sweeping up both side walls to the body of the building above. It's hard to believe a building of these proportions lacked storage space, but I can think of no other reason why on every step of the staircase, there was a case of whisky, unless the unseen storage space was already in full use.

This concert was in the presence of at least fifteen ambassadors, one of whom was the Australian ambassador. Mark, our cellist had spotted this dapper young man at the reception following the concert and was soon engaging him in conversation. I'm short at five-foot-eight, but Mark must be two or three inches shorter than me and to compensate for this lack of height, I have often observed him standing, balancing on the balls of his feet, with his legs crossed at the ankles, a position he can hold for minutes at a time. He was now holding this *Zebedee* type pose, whilst engaging in deep conversation with the ambassador who he obviously found extremely attractive. When Mark's androgens were let loose in company, he could lose all sense of decorum and just as I happened to glance across at him, I catch him digging the ambassador in the ribs with his elbow, giving him a thumbs-up and capping the performance with one of his involuntary lurches a couple of feet off to the side.

Goodbye to any notions of an Australian tour.

TWENTY-TWO

*Performing tours of the Scottish Highlands and
Islands can seem like a holiday. What a privilege!*

More than any other part of my Quartet work, nothing compared to the pleasure gained from our frequent visits to the islands of Scotland and the less travelled parts of the mainland. The trips were essentially Highland and Island tours under the guise of work; even taking the concerts into consideration, these trips could be regarded as holidays. Travelling to work through terrain that is the envy of the world and rubbing shoulders with generous and interesting people who welcomed us into their micro communities was something quite special and provided a perfect environment for making music.

Colonsay is a small island in the Inner Hebrides, three hours by boat from Oban and owned by the Strathcona family. Lord Strathcona, the Laird and music-loving patron of the arts, once organised a mini festival running over two days involving the Edinburgh Quartet exclusively. One evening concert, one lunchtime concert and one children's concert at the island's school was the full extent of the festival. In a way, it had parallels with our visits to the Middle East: both were ways of enlivening a local culture by adding a classical repertoire into a mix in which it was largely absent. If there were any hopes or fears of the island being overrun with festival goers, they would have been unfounded as the island boasts only one small hotel and very little accommodation of any other sort – and from my experience, a string quartet is not a great draw for attracting tented villages of psychedelically drugged bare-breasted men and women.

The children's concert was the most interesting from a non-musical perspective. With only one school on the island and a pupil/teacher ratio of 5/1, the solitary teacher's story could have been straight out of a Disney classic. As a teacher in the north of England for thirty years, she had always taken her annual summer holiday on Colonsay until the day the post of teacher on the island became vacant. She jumped at the chance of filling the position, applied successfully and moved to the island on one long permanently paid holiday.

Lord Strathcona entertained us in Colonsay House one afternoon and a memory lingers of this friendly and affable Laird singing the praises of Madeira wine. I can still picture him sitting enveloped in his comfortable highbacked armchair, recommending it, though I hasten to add, not for the reason in Flanders and Swann's song 'Madeira m'dear', but for its efficacious use throughout the day as a provider of sustenance.

Another children's concert of note was on the island of Sanday in the Orkney archipelago. We flew there in a four-seater aircraft, spending one night and leaving the next day after a children's concert in the morning. We were billeted with families, with Michael and I sharing a bedroom as we often did, but an odd arrangement in this case meant we could only access our room by passing through another bedroom in which two resident children slept; very homely.

Like Colonsay, Sanday had only one school, but unlike Colonsay, the pupils numbered a less remarkable forty or so, with a staff of three or four teachers. As was normal, at the end of our performance, we invited the children to ask questions which generated the predictable mildly curious interrogation of 'How long?' 'How old?' 'How many?' There was one exception from a very earnest nine-year-old who wanted to know if Hitler ever wrote any good tunes. We were unable to shed any light on this subject and happily and quickly, returned to the mundanity of the expected.

Before heading back to the mainland, the light aircraft we were now safely aboard, made a minor diversion, swooping low over the school playground where the forewarned pupils had assembled to wave goodbye.

We regularly visited Islay, another Inner Hebridean island, made famous for its distinctive malt whisky. The smoky character of the whisky derives from the peaty soil on which the island's eight distilleries sit, producing a flavour like no other Scottish whisky.

We played in a variety of venues on Islay and on this particular visit we played in the visitor's centre at the Bruichladdich distillery, our visit coinciding with the end of the most labour-intensive part of the whisky-making process.

The two events were not linked in any way, or not intended to be.

We arrived after lunch, expecting to rehearse in the afternoon as usual, to find that the room allocated for our use was being used for a celebration marking the closing of this important stage in the distillery's manufacturing process. A rehearsal in this room was going to be impossible and no other room was available. As we pondered what to do, the celebrating distillery workers gave freely of their advice, suggesting we forget our rehearsal and join in the celebrations. It was a suggestion worth contemplating as the only alternative was to find a café and kick our heels for a couple of hours. The Bruichladdich employees were persuasive and very welcoming. Seeing an opportunity to inject the party with new interest, they convinced us that their proposition was the only one worth considering.

Tables were piled high with sandwiches and soft drinks, so we were not going to go hungry or thirsty, but there was a crucial element not mentioned so far. It will come as no surprise to learn, that as the celebration was in the Bruichladdich distillery, the drink of choice was the distillery's own malt whisky. This came in unlimited quantities and on a help-yourself basis. It was a party after all, so we did imbibe but not excessively, tempering our consumption to take into account that we had a concert to perform within a few hours. If you reduce regulation to a minimum and trust people's better judgement to make the right decision, investing them with personal responsibility, it can be a real triumph of well-applied psychology. . . sometimes.

When our far-from-normal rehearsal ended and we went our separate ways, we had to decide whether to fill the remaining rehearsal time in the more orthodox manner or just make for a café. We decided, even though we hadn't overdone it, that the effects of the recently enjoyed Bruichladdich made rehearsing a rather pointless exercise and as there was still a few hours before the performance, the café option gave us adequate time with the help of a coffee or two, to be sober enough to perform much as usual.

None of us ever drank alcohol the day of a concert, so this departure from routine could have been a real disaster; happily, it was not.

The Quartet was also a frequent visitor to the Isle of Arran, with concerts taking place either in Brodick Castle or Brodick Public Hall. On one of the Brodick Hall occasions I was accosted by a stranger.

Dressed in my tails a few minutes before the concert, I decided to empty my bladder. The hall's lavatory could only be accessed from the car park because it also doubled as the village public convenience containing one of those large trough-like urinals, where the menfolk of Brodick and visitors alike could enjoy communal relief. I was in full spate when suddenly the man standing next to me issued an order in a booming voice.

'Come on Peter Markham, get a move on or you'll miss the concert.'

I turned my head, expecting to recognise some old friend trying to embarrass me, but no, he was a stranger and he was ignoring me. Standing at the trough a little further along from me was a young boy about eight, who, soon after hearing the outburst from this obviously deranged person said, 'Ok Dad, I've nearly finished.'

I had been set-up. The father's little charade had accomplished the required reaction, evidenced by my expression of bewilderment. Brandishing tickets for the concert, he informed me that from the programme, he knew that his son and I shared the same name – the only other Peter Markham I've ever met.'

At another concert, this time in Brodick Castle we were joined by the pianist Yonty Soloman in a performance of Schumann's piano quintet. Yonty had discovered that on Brodick's main street, the only newsagent cum all-purpose shop was owned and run and had been for nearly forty years, by a canny character called Tom Alexander and that he had the most amazing art collection.

Mr Alexander had at least one moment of pure genius in his life when he came up with the idea to build an art collection at little or no cost to himself (he vowed never to pay more than forty pounds for any single work). His plan was to contact as many prominent British twentieth century artists as he could think of to suggest that, as Arran had no official art gallery and ought to, he would like to take it upon himself to establish one. It was suggested to each artist that they should be represented in this venture by either donating or selling for a modest sum a work for permanent display.

The initiative had an overwhelmingly positive response and had resulted in a most extraordinary collection. Yonty had arranged weeks in advance to visit the shop and view the collection and I persuaded him to take me along too.

On entering the cluttered shop, an easily overlooked door to the left, led to Tom's flat above the shop. The extent of this collection was soon apparent, as the staircase to the flat was lined with paintings from top to bottom. The rest of the flat was no less impressive, a real treasure-trove of paintings, sculptures and ceramics of just about every British artist you could think of – with the exception being Francis Bacon, apparently the only artist to ever refuse Tom's request.

TWENTY-THREE

Enthusiasm and inexperience can be a dangerous combination. 'How many movements are there again?'

I suffered my most embarrassing moment on stage during a concert in Madrid. We were performing in the Teatro Real de Madrid, one of the great Opera Houses of the world, with a seating capacity of almost eighteen hundred. The concert was in aid of a charitable organisation and the auditorium was almost full.

A string quartet sitting on the apron, centre stage, would look lost and rather silly if the huge void behind them was left in view, so the metal fire-safety curtain had been deployed as a simple backdrop which also helped to project the sound of the quartet. This particular curtain had a small door in the corner at the foot of one of the pillars of the proscenium arch and facing the auditorium; this was our only access point to the stage.

The interval had just finished and we lined up behind

the door, waiting to enter the vast stage for the second half of the concert. A doorman is on hand and carries out his duties on cue. We pass through the door to welcoming applause and cover the enormous distance, taking several seconds before arriving centre stage. The applause continues as we take our bow and settle into our seats. It has taken me this long to notice that my music stand is naked. No music. I had been checking out a few notes during the interval and have left the music backstage. . . I have no choice. I rise, put my violin on my seat and walk as nonchalantly as possible back to the now shut handle-less little door. I feel like a complete idiot as I knock sharply on the metal door which gives off a resounding reply, then wait. It's apparent that the doorman is no longer at his post as an inordinate amount of time passes before it eventually opens and more time accumulates while I locate my music. I now have to repeat my journey in reverse. Passing through the door for a second time, I'm greeted with thunderous applause from a bemused audience as I emerge from backstage and repeat my lengthy trek back to centre stage clutching my music, evidence of the reason for my solo perambulation for all to see (I'd swear the distance has increased since the beginning of the concert). Before sitting down, I indulge in a massively overindulgent bow, drawing the Gerard Hoffnungish farcical episode to its conclusion.

An extraordinary aberration on my part, created a more professionally embarrassing moment when starting the second half of a concert in Inverness with Brahms' third quartet in B flat major, a work very familiar to me. It was the only piece in the second half and it begins with a two-bar duo between violin two and viola. The duo pivots around the note F natural in the 2nd violin part; well, normally it's an F natural, but on this occasion it was an F sharp, as for some inexplicable reason I decided to transpose my part into the key of D major with the addition of a single B natural helping to make a convincing transposition. When the entire quartet came together in the third bar and the music reverted to the correct key, the clunk on the senses was absolutely staggering. My colleagues were thunderstruck at my colossal invention, but it took a few seconds of confusion on my part for it to fully register that it was my descent into near criminal activity that had been responsible for this outrageous act!

I did take some solace in the notion that Brahms' 3rd, of his three string quartets is acknowledged as being his most humorous. . .

Audience members suffer embarrassments too. The most embarrassing one I recall occurred in Salvador Dali's hometown of Figueres in Catalonia. The occasion was a late-night performance for the local festival, with the festival's young director very much in evidence. He was new to the role and his enthusiasm verged on hysteria, doing anything he could to be noticed. Our final piece was a late Beethoven quartet, opus 132, a quartet in five movements rather than the more normal four, a fact the attention-seeking director was oblivious to. On completion of movement four, he jumped to his feet in boisterous fashion and applauded loudly. The remaining Figueres audience were better informed than this young man – or they had read their programme notes more carefully –

and did not follow his lead. The director was left stranded in limbo while his blunder hit home and a very red-faced and embarrassed young man sunk back on his seat in a cacophony of silence.

He certainly got his quota of attention that day.

The most embarrassing moment for someone on the platform, but not one of the players was delivered by Betty. Betty, at almost eighty years of age, was a regular page turner for the pianist Yonty Solomon, but it was hard to know exactly why.

I think she must have established herself as Yonty's page turner when in Scotland over a period of many years and gained some form of squatter's rights to the chair. She also acted as his chauffeur, provider of sandwiches and flasks of tea and carrier of his music, but as the years caught up with her, her expertise at page turning waned. Yonty seemed willing to put up with her ineptitude as long as she could still successfully provide, fetch and carry.

In this performance of Schumann's piano quintet at Peebles Hydro Hotel, we could clearly hear Yonty, bad-temperedly giving Betty audible instructions on when to turn the pages. These are so loud that it was impossible for the audience not to pick them up. The whole performance was peppered with variations on a theme of, 'Now, NOW.' or 'No. NOT NOW.'

As poor Betty became ever more flustered, bobbing up and down on her seat to turn, or not turn the pages, her panicky movements were being transferred to her chair, which was slowly but surely being nudged backwards, until in the middle of one of the movements, Betty was no longer in a position to take instructions, having fallen off the podium from a height of about half a metre. It was quite a commotion and of course the performance came to a halt. She was unhurt and able to continue, with little sympathy from a scowling and rather precious Yonty who was soon back in full flow, 'Now. NOW.'

An all-round embarrassing situation arose on a trip to Barcelona when giving a children's concert in the beautiful and unique 'Palau de la Música Catalana'. None of the Quartet spoke Spanish, so a Spanish actor who spoke no English had been engaged to present the show. Supplied with a script in Spanish, she had to introduce each piece with a little explanation, followed by us performing the relevant piece: a series of chat, play, chat, play. The hidden danger of the arrangement was that we didn't know what she was saying and she, having no musical knowledge, didn't know what we were playing. Halfway through the concert, we played a piece in two sections and between the sections, she mistakenly spoke. As we were not familiar with the script, we presumed her mistaken interruption was part of the script, when it was actually the introduction to the next piece and so from that point to the end of the concert, synchronisation between music and spoken word was out by one step. We had a fair idea that something like this was happening but ploughed on regardless. The most confusing moment came when we launched into the last piece unexpectantly, as the piece before was thought to have been our final piece.

I was reminded of the Two Ronnies Mastermind sketch,

where the contestant chooses to answer questions on the question before last.

As a favour, we did once perform Shostakovich's eighth string quartet for our host in Jeddah and him alone, but the *bona fide* concert with the smallest audience we ever played to was a little more surreal.

We had been booked by Joan, the manager of a large NHS hospital in the suburbs of London, to give a surprise concert in honour of her ex-mother-in-law's eightieth birthday. Joan had gone to great lengths to conceal the concert from Doris, although Doris was anticipating some kind of celebration. Doris lived close to Dunblane and to be able to continue the deception until the concert, our rehearsal had been organised to take place in Dunblane Cathedral hall in the afternoon, with further instructions telling us where to go for the evening performance. The programme was specific in that two pieces should be played, one of which had to be Schubert's great C major string quintet (quartet plus extra cello) and a quartet of our own choosing. The Schubert quintet had been requested because it was the favourite piece of both Doris and her late husband.

After our rehearsal and wearing our tails, we set off from Dunblane. Fifteen miles or so later, as we approached the address, we started looking for what we presumed will be a large house, or small hall, or something similar. We were surprised to find the address led us to a simple stone-built cottage with dormer windows, one in a terrace of four on a small country road. The door was opened by Joan who ushered us quietly into the living room where there was a table piled high with birthday fare, with pride of place given to an elegant birthday cake made by Joan and lovingly coddled on the back seat of her car on her overnight drive from London.

We prepared ourselves for the concert with Joan instructing us to follow her up the stairs to the room above once she had had enough time to seat herself. With instruments in one hand and music stands and music in the other, we mounted the stairs and surfaced in a converted attic space to applause from an audience of two. . .

It really made slight difference whether we played to two, or one-thousand-and-two*, especially when there was an opportunity to perform Schubert's string quintet and we gave it our all.

The peculiarity of the day had one last element. As part of our agreement with Joan, it had been arranged that we would stay on after our performance and celebrate Doris' birthday as her honoured guests: I found it strange and rather sad, that someone at the age of eighty had only an ex-daughter-in-law and a *rent-a-crowd* with whom to celebrate this milestone, but foraging for an explanation right then didn't

---

*We did almost play to an audience of zero in Dornoch, the small town with a cathedral on the northeast coast of Scotland. We turned up to find that the concert had been advertised for the next day, but as this was one of several consecutive concerts, we would have been performing elsewhere that day. Fortunately, the cathedral wasn't being used the day of our arrival, so while we rehearsed, a local volunteer spent the afternoon on the phone, drumming up a handful of people to make up a last-minute audience. I was even able to play a part in swelling the audience, as my parents were with me during this tour.

seem appropriate. The strange circumstances of course didn't affect our participation and my foraging was focused in a more pertinent direction as I set about decimating the birthday fare spread out on the living room table, helping to play my part in conjuring up a party atmosphere.

By the time it came to leave, we thanked a happy slightly tipsy and tearful Doris and a caring and considerate Joan, leaving them to slip quietly back into their private lives.

TWENTY-FOUR

*'To mislay your Quartet's 1st violin once may be
regarded as a misfortune; to mislay him twice...'*

Early October 1995, the Quartet was preparing for a concentrated touring period in Europe, followed almost immediately by ten days of touring in Scotland. The European tour would begin in England, going on to France, Germany and Holland, with a couple more performances in England on the return journey. For practical reasons our only choice was to travel by road and for financial reasons a single car would have to suffice. Unfortunately, covering long distances cooped up in one car for three weeks isn't the best way to cement relationships that were already under strain.

I am afraid Miles' chain-smoking and general way of life were rapidly catching up with him; it was affecting his playing in ways obvious to us and our audiences. Performances were marred by inconsistencies, significant blemishes and lethargy. His heart was most definitely not in it and his apparent lack of concern for his unreliable playing suggested all was not well. Newspaper critics were not slow to pick up on this, with the most recent reviews never more than tolerable in their praise.

Miles Baster's name was synonymous with the Edinburgh Quartet since its formation in 1959 and his longevity of tenure had been a significant influence on the ever-improving Scottish music scene and the reputation and success of the Edinburgh Quartet. Given his monumental part in the EQ's history and our long collaboration, Michael and I were finding it a particularly sensitive situation to deal with; Mark on the other hand appeared to have few such qualms. Throughout the tour, it wasn't unusual for him to rather callously accuse Miles of his shortcomings during intervals and after concerts. By the time we got back to Edinburgh, things were at an all-time low and a couple of free days back in Scotland were more than welcome before we had to hit the road again.

For the Scottish tour, it was not necessary for us to cram into one car, we could afford the luxury of taking three cars, giving me the independence to fill what would be an abundance of free time in any way I chose. I was very happy to be back in the world I loved best, nowhere near a European motorway, or queueing at a time-consuming exit point to cross the English Channel.

Things felt a little better now we had reconnected with what made us feel most rooted. Even Miles had a bit of spring back in his playing: a convivial night out at 'Bar Italia' on Lothian Road was no doubt responsible for that.

However, the recharging did not take long to run down

again. The issue was too serious and pervasive; it would not simply disappear by having a few days off. The atmosphere deteriorated to something similar to that of the European tour, with Miles withdrawing into himself more and more, Miles was never that communicative, but now this was different.

Mark was still insensitively snapping away, with Mike and I, through a mix of emotional confusion and weakness of character, still unable to find a way to approach him, so by the time we arrived back in Edinburgh again, things were decidedly not good.

November 8th, the day after our return, we had a lunchtime concert in Hutcheson's Hall, Glasgow which unsurprisingly, did not go well. After the concert, we scheduled our next rehearsal for the following day and went our separate ways, three of us back to Edinburgh and Miles to an afternoon of teaching at the Royal Scottish Academy of Music and Drama – and we never saw him again.

We convened for a rehearsal on the 9th without Miles and with no information to explain his non-appearance. Over the next few days every effort was made to contact him, all to no avail. He'd had a landline phone installed in the last few years but ringing him produced no response nor did knocking on his flat door, which remained firmly shut. None of his friends that we knew of had heard anything from him. His only living family member, a sister in Woking had also heard nothing.

This second Miles disappearance was immediately more concerning than the time of his window smashing episode,

> Evening News, Saturday, November 17, 1984
>
> **THE MORNINGSIDES**

as it was quite clear when last seen, that he was suffering from some deep-rooted mental anguish. Everyone was extremely worried and with the police now involved, the time came to force entry to his flat in Gilmerton. To general relief, Miles was not there; better to still be missing than lying comatose, or worse.

At the same time all this was going on, the Quartet had professional commitments to fulfil, the first on the Isle of Skye within three days of Miles' disappearance. Skye Music Club were given the option to cancel or postpone, but was adamant that the gig should be honoured, as locating and contacting all those who had already purchased tickets would be an impossibility in their far-flung community. One of the pieces we were scheduled to play was a sextet for string quartet, small pipes and percussion, composed by the young Scottish musician Martyn Bennet, who was also to be the small pipes player.

Before our recent touring, a goodly number of rehearsals with Miles had already taken place on this sextet. Without him and with too little time to find a replacement and start rehearsing this tricky piece anew, the sextet could not be performed. Fortunately, Martyn was a violinist having studied with Miles at the Academy so we contacted Skye Music Club and suggested an alternative programme. With next to no rehearsal time available, we offered the club a completely revamped programme, cobbled together from a more easily assimilated repertoire and performed by the existing quintet of players.

The club agreed and with Martyn's willingness to play 2nd violin to my first, coupled with his innate musicianship, we gave them a concert comprising two string quartets and an improvisation for percussion and pipes, which went down surprisingly well, leaving a contented audience to wend their various ways home.

A week later, we had one more commitment to execute before we would be in a position to replace Miles with either a temporary 1st violin, or someone on trial for the permanent position.

I was not finding it easy to step up so suddenly from 2nd violin to 1st, but life was made easier with encouragement from my colleagues, who included for this concert, Robert McFall deputising as 2nd violin and pianist Murray McLachlan in a performance of Schumann's piano quintet. Mark on the other hand was less encouraging, which came as no surprise. Right from the beginning of our working relationship when his impersonation of Charles Hawtrey could transform a rehearsal into a scene from 'Carry On Up The Crotchet', we never really got on. This concert, despite Mark's lack of cooperation, also passed muster.

The search for Miles continued. Concern mounted when after breaking into his flat, the only thing that appeared to be missing was his violin. His clothes, furniture, books and music were in place and everything looked as though he might walk through the door at any moment. Miles was now officially listed as a Missing Person. Three weeks went by with not a word or sign of his whereabouts.

Then, at the end of November, there was a transaction on Miles' bank card at an ATM in Penzance. From this single transaction, the police were able to trace him and discover him safe and well and living in Cornwall. We knew that Miles had been evacuated to Cornwall during the war. He had been billeted with a couple who more than likely provided him with a home life he probably never experienced with his biological parents. In his hour of need, he had returned to the very same couple, now in their late eighties.

Can spontaneously disappearing be a genetic condition? Or perhaps a condition empathetically triggered by friends? Miles' father disappeared in very mysterious circumstances when Miles was a young man. He was a lawyer in London and when the police searched his office after he had vanished without trace, they found he had only one set of clients: the

Kray twins. It was commonly supposed at the time that murder was the reason for his unexplained disappearance. However, decades later in about 1990, Miles told me that he had just been contacted by the police, who informed him that his father had recently died in Australia – his identity confirmed from dental records – where he had been living under an assumed name for all those intervening years.

And there's the case of Adrian, a member of Edinburgh's Century Club. In the days when pub closing time in Scotland was 10pm, locals would find novel ways of drinking socially beyond that hour. Before I joined the quartet in 1975, Miles was already part of a group devoted to this pursuit. It consisted of a collection of like-minded *gentlemen* who had banded together and bought a property in Dublin Street for the sole purpose of drinking after hours. They called it the Century Club installing a caretaker/barman in a flat within the property. The members – each one owned an equal share – plus their guests could go there and drink to their heart's content, within the law. Some years before Miles disappeared, Adrian, a friend of his and paid-up member of the Century Club, left his wife at home one day and was missing for several weeks before turning up in the Channel Islands never to return. He was also a professional musician.

After his disappearance following that lunchtime concert in Glasgow in 1995, Miles never made contact with any member of the quartet again and, as far as I know, this was reciprocated. He lived on in Cornwall, spending his time teaching and performing concertos with local amateur orchestras until his death from cancer in 2004.

Finding a replacement for Miles was not a procedure to look forward to. Applicants' existing commitments had to be accommodated and arrangements were often complicated and impractical. Trial periods were frequently fragmented, with some players' trials overlapping others. Sometimes the same piece was being rehearsed with different players for performances on different days. I think the strangest part for me was the detailed rehearsing of familiar pieces, almost entirely for the benefit of the 1st violin.

The position attracted an eclectic mix of aspiring quartet players for a variety of reasons, some for the pure love of chamber music, through to a means of escape from a lifetime of regimented orchestral playing. As well as their playing, a great variation in age and diversity of personal circumstances made choosing far from easy, taking a full year before a new 1st violin was appointed.

One unsuccessful applicant is worth documenting, Peter M Tanfield (appropriately known as PMT to use his own words). Confident doesn't begin to describe him. At thirty-six, he is sixteen years my junior, but imbued with a self-belief that has taken at least fifty years to cultivate. I'm envious. It only takes until the third day of rehearsals for a less attractive facet of his character to present itself offering a clue as to what working with him might entail. He tells me to stop talking when he is talking. I had not been talking *over* him, I had merely been discussing in muted tones, a musical point with Michael while, at the same time, he had been doing something similar with Mark. I'm flabbergasted. I fight my corner, only to be met with complete indifference.

As far as I can make out, PMT has never held a full-time job, preferring to freelance until one of his attempts to gain a position commensurate with his notion of his own worth pays off. He told me of one such effort coming unstuck when a trial for concert master of an American orchestra foundered the day before his first rehearsal, because he fell over in the bath and broke his leg.

As a freelance player from I believe a privileged background, he chooses not to work that often making him relatively free and able to give us lengthy periods of his time. We have a three-week American tour coming up, a regular event occurring every four years, so it's 'fortunate' that Peter is available to do the whole tour. The tour culminates in a concert, which will also be broadcast live on national radio and will take place in the National Gallery of Art in Washington. The programme has been chosen from a shortlist of pieces given to us by the promoters, which consists exclusively of pieces by contemporary American composers. The work that finishes the first half of the concert is by Ruth Crawford Seeger and the third movement is a complete nightmare to play, a slow movement marked Larghetto. Each of the four players plays a series of very long slow notes with each note having a crescendo and decrescendo throughout, but all four players start and finish their notes at separate times. Therein lies the problem because without a beat there is no way of knowing where each player is in relation to the others. Our solution is that PMT will tap his foot inaudibly at the beginning of each bar and in this way we will at least always know when each bar begins.

We make sure at the beginning of the movement that we all have good sight lines to Peter's right foot as he taps out the first bar, second, third. . . where is the fourth? There is no fourth, or subsequent bars either. The third bar is the very last to be honoured with acknowledgement but Peter plays on regardless. He doesn't take his eyes off his music and offers no alternative help. I can't imagine what he's thinking. The rest of us flounder along, pretending to know what we are doing, dutifully swelling on notes of indeterminate length. My colleagues are stunned, they appear traumatised, so after what seems an acceptable amount of time, I decide enough is enough. It is obvious that nobody knows what to do, so through body movement I indicate to the others that I have started playing my final note. Amazingly this is picked up and we finish the movement in convincing style with a lengthy decrescendo followed by an exaggerated silence. With perspiration now flowing freely, we gather ourselves before confidently tackling the more approachable fourth movement, drawing the first half of the performance to a close.

To make things worse, the concert is being covered by the critic emeritus of the *Washington Post*, who is sitting in the front row with a colleague and following our progress via the score that's resting on his knees. He is sitting so close, that at times I'm aware of him turning pages and pointing out things in the score to his companion.

As we leave the stage and enter the dressing room, an almighty row breaks out between Mark and Peter which must be clearly heard in the auditorium. Mark is furious at the lack of footwork from Peter, screaming uncontrollably at him. Peter stays relatively calm and typically refuses to take any responsibility for the debacle.

After many weeks of working with PMT, I have long ago decided I can't work with this man, but up until this point, Michael and Mark have been seriously in favour of offering him the job. The Washington concert is the last of the tour and the last commitment we have with Peter for some weeks. He is now heading for Italy from New York and the three of us are flying home out of Washington, which gives us our first opportunity in Peter's absence to discuss his suitability for 1st violin. Fortunately, Ruth Crawford Seeger has come to my aid and my two colleagues concede that this incident is enough to exclude him from further consideration.

Back in Scotland two weeks later, we receive a copy of the *Washington Post's* criticism. The opening paragraph is along these lines, *Is it not time that America had a string quartet that can do justice to our national composers to the same extent as the Edinburgh Quartet?* and then goes on to sing our praises in a similar vein for the entire programme.

Considering the presence of scores, shrieking from the dressing room and an unofficial improvised movement, this is extraordinary.

As for PMT, a few years later he ended up leading the Australian Quartet for a brief period, before settling down in Tasmania with academic life becoming his main occupation. His confidence appears undiminished as I noticed on the internet that he was a finalist in 'Australian of the Year' in 2008.

TWENTY-FIVE

Changing professional direction can be very dependent on the prevailing wind. 'That looks like a storm to me.'

Within twelve months of Miles' disappearance in 1995, the quartet's emotional stability was once again sorely tested, when an incident of even greater significance occurred. Michael's family suffered a devastating tragedy. In the autumn of 1996 Janie, Michael's wife and mother of their four children (the youngest only seven-years-old) was killed in a car crash.

Janie's death, like any tragic sudden death, had an instantaneous impact, with immediate family and close friends rallying round Michael and his distraught and disbelieving children as the household tried to continue living a reasonably normal existence.

All our rehearsals now took place in Michael's house and since Christopher left the Quartet, Michael had been in all but name, the Quartet's administrator. Besides the rehearsal room, a second room was taken over as the Quartet's office and with the help of Fiona, an energetic and diligent part time administrator, assisted occasionally by Ken the retired bank manager, the Quartet continued functioning as usual. This meant that people, other than those helping out with the family, were also coming and going, a situation which perhaps helped to distract and connect the family to a world outside its present sadness.

At the same time, the Quartet was still in the process of looking for a replacement for Miles. This often involved those on trial having lengthy periods in Edinburgh at their own expense, which could for some applicants, result in the outlay of serious sums of money on top of losing income from work they might otherwise have been doing. Michael and his large house once again came to the rescue. Since the beginning of the search for a new 1st violin, Michael had generously been providing accommodation in his home for those requiring it and this continued after Janie's death.

We finally made an appointment. Jane Murdoch was officially our new 1st violin as from January 8th, 1997. We knew Jane as a student at the RSAM&D in Glasgow and as a colleague when beginning her professional career in Scotland; she was now a twenty-nine-year-old single parent of a three-year-old daughter moving up from London.

It must have been a strange time for both she and Michael during their individual crises. Michael's long journey in coming to terms with his family nightmare continued and Jane's battle for custody of her very young child can't have been easy at this demanding time in her professional life.

It was beginning to feel a little strange for me too. Jane was benefitting from Michael's generosity, living in his house with her daughter and developing a strong bond wth him. Additionally, Mark lived alone nearby and was spending almost all his leisure time in their company. I had no wish to socialise with my colleagues and was being made to feel more and more like a killjoy for not doing so.

Rehearsals were becoming sporadic, with a sense of 'Let's get them over with as quickly as possible'. This attitude was rapidly changing an established and acceptable working practice into something so light and casual that pieces were no longer being properly prepared. Standards suffered and it wasn't long before we paid the price for this cavalier approach during a performance of demanding contemporary works in Odense, Denmark.

The concert is a live broadcast on Danish radio and in preparation, our rehearsals have been careless and flippant, with the whole programme under-rehearsed. In the middle of one of the pieces, I become aware of a certain amount of discomfort underway to my right, followed soon after by Jane whispering in my direction 'Where are we?' (meaning, where in the music? not in which city). I ignore this plea as, from experience, on the rare occasions when I've lost my place when taking my eyes off the music for too long, I have always quickly found my place again. This performance is not so fortunate and it's not long before I hear a second appeal for help, this one sounding a little more frantic, with a hint of underlying chortling detectable. Jane is playing, but only now and then, interpolating suitably sounding collections of notes to give the impression all is normal. She is obviously nowhere near finding her place on the page, so I try pointing with the scroll of my violin to an approaching rehearsal letter on my music. I can see this is not going to work, so I resort to joining the general conversation and mutter the rehearsal letter as quietly as I can. Success. After a few more seconds of improvisation while Jane gets her bearings, we are complete once more.

The interval soon follows, but far from being a moment in which to reflect on what was almost an embarrassing disaster, the incident is brushed off and treated as a cause for great amusement.

The near fiasco reminded me of a couple of similar incidents from earlier days when both Miles and Michael, during separate concerts, turned their music over at the end of a piece to find their last pages missing, with both players producing quite different reactions, outcomes and attitude to those on display in Odense.

In Miles' case, the last movement of Borodin's second quartet was the piece in question. Although I was aware something was slightly amiss, he executed such a convincing job that I was unaware that there was a whole page missing. I would guess that no one in the audience noticed anything was wrong.

Michael's test came with Dvorak's American Quartet and his response was even more impressive. He delivered a note-perfect rendition of his final page without a flicker of panic or discomfort.

It's no surprise that those particular two pieces were the

ones with pages missing as they happen to be the two most popular pieces in the quartet repertoire, the Borodin for the familiarity of the two themes in the slow movement, one of which occurs in his second symphony and the other in the musical 'Kismet'. The popularity of the Dvorak simply stems from it being easy listening – concise, lively, tuneful and happy, the result of some very clever composing.

But tension within the Quartet was not necessarily a negative influence on our performance. Relationships ebbed and flowed and communication, usually between the same characters could influence moods for lengthy periods, with unresolved musical interpretation often at the core of conflict. Returning to our shabby hotel after a mediocre performance in Cardiff in 1993 we settled in at the hotel bar. An air of pent-up emotions had been pervading the atmosphere since the end of the concert and it didn't take too long for the conversation to come round to discussing our performance, something we rarely did immediately after playing. Oblique references and gentle criticism were at first quite tolerable, but as the alcohol flowed and the evening lengthened, personal accusations started flying about and the possibility of anything constructive being proposed was totally lost.

We were by now well under the influence of our refreshment and it was getting late. I decided that nothing but damage could be accomplished by prolonging the evening and, having made my opinion known, I went to bed; but not before Mark was able to throw in a few remarks along the lines of 'That's right, just run away if you don't like what you are hearing' and 'Chicken'.

Next morning revealed that the trio had carried on drinking well after my departure, particularly evidenced by Michael's alarming greyish hue and were in no fit state to face a car journey the length of Wales.

What the day had in store for us was daunting by any standards, let alone when nursing a hangover. A drive to Rhyl, a three-hour-rehearsal and a demanding programme of Bartok, late Beethoven and a contemporary work by William Mathias, in the composer's presence. The journey lived up to expectations, with several emergency stops to allow one of our number to throw up.

On arrival in Rhyl and with the rehearsal underway, something unexpected happened. Little was said, which was to be expected, but the playing had a distinct element of competitiveness. It soon became obvious that each of us was trying to prove to all the others that he was the better player/musician.

This childlike determination to excel spilled over into the evening performance in an even more exaggerated way, with everyone playing their hearts out, producing one of the best concerts I can remember.

The relationships in our new formation were getting no better as the months went by and I was really feeling out of place in this new set-up with Jane. Excluded, uncomfortable and unhappy, it was quite apparent that I had to make a choice whether to stay and strive to resolve the burgeoning problems or leave. I was loathe to do anything in haste.

Then in May 1998, matters were taken out of my hands. Behind the scenes, machinations had been underway to such a degree that unbeknown to me, my replacement had already been auditioned and I was presented with a *fait accompli* dressed up as concerned criticism from my three colleagues. I realised, reading between the lines as their message was being delivered, that I was being given no choice but to resign.

The complexion of my membership of the Edinburgh Quartet had now taken on a distinctly different hue and contemplating continuing to work with antagonistic and duplicitous colleagues was something I couldn't possibly do, making my once attractive employment untenable. As a small gesture of defiance in the hope of creating some frustration, I delayed acquiescing for a week before handing in my resignation. When I did, I stated that mid-August, after our annual Aberdeen International Youth Festival residency had taken place, should be my final commitment to the Quartet and this was accepted.

As I write that last paragraph, an excerpt from Bach's St. Matthew Passion has just burst from the radio. The excerpt is '*Erbarme dich, mein Gott*'. It seems to encapsulate the sadness of the moment even though the circumstance was entirely different.

I was deeply sorry that I had to give up a way of life I loved so much, but it was definitely for the best whatever the future might hold. Leaving the Quartet after twenty-three years was dramatic enough in itself, but other life-changing events were on their way.

I was now facing a drop of seventy-five percent in my

earnings and at fifty-three-years-old, finding new sources of income might not be so easy. My knees were knackered and about to bring an end to those halcyon twenty years of running. And within the year, I was to embark on separation from my long-term partner of thirty-three years, sell the family home and move to a yet unknown location.

TWENTY-SIX

*The ever-lucky 2nd violin can find a silver lining,
even love, in teaching and far-off Hungary.*

My new life after EQ shifted away from being one that was predominantly that of a performer to one which was more orientated around teaching. Unfortunately, my work with the Scottish Chamber Orchestra came to an end as, after an acrimonious separation, it became impossible for my estranged partner and I to work within close proximity to one another without all hell breaking loose.

My membership of the Scottish Ballet Orchestra provided sparse seasonal work which I was glad of, plus a number of freelance orchestral gigs throughout the year. This was the sum of my performing. I had joined the orchestra of Scottish Ballet in 1997 with a degree of reluctance, doing so because the rest of the EQ had already joined the previous year. Their membership had created a situation where quartet rehearsals had been relegated to a role of secondary importance to that of the ballet schedule, leaving me high and dry whenever the ballet was operating, so becoming a member myself was a practical solution to ending my idleness. It also gave me the opportunity to play many performances of Romeo and Juliet by Prokofiev, which I think is one of the greatest pieces of music ever written. Remarkable orchestration with not a superfluous note throughout.

After fifteen years of membership a very odd thing happened. During the 2012-13 season, out of the blue, myself and most of the older members of the orchestra were afflicted by a strange phenomenon. We suddenly found that we could no longer play to the required standard. This unseen, invidious invader was complicated however, in that this loss of ability was only detectable by two or three people, but not by those musicians concerned. Naturally, the situation needed to be addressed immediately and one by one, we older players were interviewed by the acting principal conductor and the Leader of the orchestra, both of whom were fortunate enough to be able to hear and register our sudden decline in the required standard. We were then told of our mysterious and unaccountable deterioration and given a trial period in which to improve. You can imagine what a terrible shock this was, especially as we had to improve without being able to recognise what was wrong in the first place.

It was a very unsettling time, resulting in some players not surprisingly failing to ever comprehend how to improve and just giving up and resigning; others fought hard, but finally succumbed to the stress created by this invisible and pernicious interloper and some, like myself, were lucky enough to survive and play another day. Those of us who did survive, puzzlingly, never discovered how and in what way we managed to improve sufficiently in order to retain our positions.

There was a mutation to this phenomenon. Two older members who had managed to escape being afflicted by this insidious presence were shortly afterwards hit by an equally strange manifestation, compelling them to transgress the rules of Scottish Ballet's orchestral contract inexplicably and uncharacteristically and although the infringements in both cases were minor, (the players had been members for about twenty years) the orchestra's management seemed to be under the spell of an equally odd compulsion and dismissed them without a scintilla of flexibility or consideration for their years of loyal service. All very strange indeed.

This sudden loss of personnel on such a grand scale could have dealt a devastating blow to the orchestra, the violin sections in particular, but fortunately the orchestra's Leader was able to come to the rescue. With the assistance of the vastly knowledgeable fixer, the Leader was able to offer a selection of her students and ex-students the opportunity to gain invaluable professional experience by shoring up the violin sections. Some players were even privileged enough to do so without having the necessity of attending a rehearsal.

On the teaching side following my departure from the Edinburgh Quartet, I retained my post at the Royal Scottish Academy of Music & Drama and took on an extra one at a private school in St. Andrews. I did that for a year until the Head of Music told me she had to rewrite all my school reports as they were too negative, offering the explanation that as the school relied heavily on the funds accrued from individual instrumental lessons, only comments that would encourage parents to continue pressing their reluctant offspring to have lessons would suffice. Not a workplace ethic I was willing to be part of any longer.

With my usual good luck, I was offered and gratefully accepted a post at the City of Edinburgh Music School. One door opening as another closed. Teaching at the school over the next fourteen years was by far the most rewarding work I did during this period: talented pupils, a caring and productive staff and great working conditions encouraged my slow but sure conversion from performer to teacher.

At the beginning of this time of transition, I was feeling quite disconnected and a little lost, but slowly, over several years, as the pieces started to fall into place, that sense of deracination was replaced and an anchored existence was once more realised. I found a wonderful house in the countryside, one of eleven in a Victorian terrace next to the main Edinburgh/Glasgow railway line, with a view beyond of the everchanging beauty of the Campsie Fells. Looking out from my living room bay window, I would often daydream as the ever-present westerlies constantly changed the vista. The small hamlet of Dullatur in which the house stands is close to Stirling and made a perfect base for my commitments in both Edinburgh and Glasgow.

I then took on another teaching post at Glenalmond

College in Perthshire, giving my working week a full and very regular structure with holiday periods clearly designated well in advance, quite different from the ever-changing work schedule that was operated by the Quartet. In my thirty years as a performer, travel had been an integral part of my work and I saw holiday periods as a time to stay put, but with this change of circumstance, I also viewed travel in a different light. All my work now being of a domestic nature, I saw my free time as a chance to get out there and pester my friends far and wide. This included a month Euro-railing in Eastern Europe in 2000 which took me to Hungary where I spent some days with Bogi and family and an abiding memory of one of my all-time favourite pop songs ringing out from every shop, restaurant and coffee bar in the region – Sunny Afternoon by the Kinks

As recounted in the opening pages, the romantic side of my life was revived in April 2007 with the arrival of Boglárka's letter inviting me to Szeged for the summer. Sára and I got married in 2013 on the beach in Onekaka, a small hamlet of alternative souls, set in the north-western region of South Island, New Zealand, known as Golden Bay. At the heart of this collection of smallholdings stands the iconic 'Mussel Inn', an unofficial Community Centre masquerading as a pub/micro-brewery/restaurant/performance space/kids play area/job centre and much more. We chose Onekaka as my son Dominic now lives there with his wife Sarah and their two children and works in the micro-brewery.

I started dividing my time between Scotland and Hungary, spending all available free time in Szeged with Sára who works as a state prosecutor. Since she still has many more working years ahead of her, naturally enough Hungary is our home.

I continued working full time in Scotland, although I did make a tentative approach to find work with the Szeged orchestra when first spending substantial periods of time there. I was adamant that I wouldn't accept work which might take employment away from a lowly paid local player. I was simply interested in being part of a professional performance, suggesting I could be used to boost up a section that might otherwise not happen and no remuneration would be necessary.

My approach was enthusiastically received, but a combination of laziness and reticence at having to play through a few Beethoven sonatas with the principal conductor before being engaged resulted in me not taking up the offer and the opportunity slipped away.

Instead, I prefer to help swell the audience numbers of the many performances we attend in Szeged and Budapest. One concert in Szeged had a particular resonance to an incident that had taken place shortly after I had left the EQ, the details of which had come down to me via the grapevine.

The EQ are rehearsing on the day of a concert in a rural location somewhere in Scotland. Included in the programme is a piano quintet with Gusztáv Fenyö as pianist. Gusztáv is familiar to members of the Quartet as he's a resident of Glasgow and has collaborated with us in the past.

A piano is unavailable at the venue and so an electric keyboard is the only alternative. Compared to a decent piano, playing an electric keyboard is a torturous experience for any concert pianist, without in this case, the pianist having the added annoyance of a petulant cellist breathing down his neck, endlessly criticising his every move. On top of that, Mark's criticisms are ill-founded. What he's mostly complaining about is entirely down to the fundamental limitations of an electric keyboard.

Eventually Gusztáv, a hot-blooded Hungarian, can take no more of these churlish interruptions and with Mark now leaning over his shoulder and niggardly pointing out some issue in the piano part for the umpteenth time, Gusztáv rises from his piano stool and executes a perfect right cross full to the face of a much subdued and disconcerted cellist.

It turns out that the grapevine had relayed the incident in reliable detail, as the account was corroborated by Gusztáv many years later when I go backstage at a concert in the Szeged Music Conservatorium where he is about to perform.

As I don't work in Hungary, much of my abundant free time is spent cycling on the empty country roads around Szeged, with occasional forays across the border into Serbia. One ill-advised trip nearly ended in an international incident when I crossed the Serbian border riding atop the river Tisza embankment, which is part of the area's flood defences. I was without passport or any other form of identification and was unaware of my transgression until nabbed by border guards as I re-entered Hungary. Luckily, I guess the authorities at the other end of the guard's mobile phones thought it not worth the bureaucratic hassle an arrest would entail and after twenty minutes the guards angrily waved me on.

Apart from cycling, my main source of exercise, learning Hungarian is another rewarding if frustrating use of time. After an initial few years of reasonably assiduous effort learning the language is now an intermittent activity with not a great deal to show for it; each attempt these days is like trying to locate the thread on a poorly engineered jar by first turning the lid in the opposite direction.

And of course, my violin, now played infrequently, continues to be a constant, the instrument which links together everything that has happened throughout my life.

Theme and Variations

Theme and Variations

ACKNOWLEDGEMENTS

Before acknowledging those who have helped with writing this book, I would like to voice my appreciation of some of the many generous and kindly folk who gave their unconditional help and support to the Edinburgh Quartet during my lengthy and charmed membership.

The low paid, and in some cases unpaid help with administration of Fiona Ward, Ken Main and Bert Davis in Edinburgh, and Irene Addison in Aberdeen was invaluable.

Thanks also go to the stalwart members of The Edinburgh Quartet Trust, which consisted of Michael, Charlie, John, George, and Gerald for all the time and thought they put in.

Our own concert promotions in Edinburgh required a small number of dedicated helpers who could always be relied upon to man the doors and deal with any necessary catering. Without the unpaid help of Alex Dickie, Susan Emslie, and James Beyer over many years, this would have been impossible.

People's homes often became open houses for the

travelling EQ, with board and lodging freely provided, and friendships made, so I want to thank in particular some of those I remember well: Margaret and Jumbo Wakefield on Skye, Jumbo, an imposing military man of impressive proportions as his nickname implies, will always be remembered for dropping a full tray of dirty crockery behind a half open door connecting the kitchen to the church hall (that evening's venue) just after the second half of our concert had begun! Their hospitality was carried on by their daughter, Deidre and husband Bill after their deaths.

Barbara Myatt and her ever-bowtie-attired husband, Leslie in their remote but warm home in Halkirk near Thurso.

Ethel Walker and husband David in their converted mill in Argyllshire, full of antiques, and Ethel's wonderful paintings.

Douglas Henderson, curator at Inverewe Gardens, and his wife, Margaret.

Fiona and Ken Way at Trebost on Mull in their cosy wood-built farmhouse.

Jean and Andy Leonard on Orkney, Mary and Norman Wetherick in Aberdeen, and many many more...

I am in still in contact with some, in particular Christian and Anne Spickermann in Ahrensburg, my hosts for the first time nearly forty years ago when performing in their town. I now count them as two of my closest friends, meeting regularly and even taking holidays together.

As for the book, thanks must go to Susan Emslie for encouraging me to put pen to paper (which in reality was how the enterprise got underway). Having had her ear bent on so many occasions, her suggestion to write down the tales was probably only a ruse to escape further bombardment...

Thanks also to Polly, my daughter for giving it the first once-over, and David Kerr for offering expert guidance.

A final thank you to Sean Bradley of Thirsty Books for his invaluable insights when overseeing this project.

The author welcomes comments or general communications from readers by email: Petermarkhammemoir@gmail.com